THE NAZI EXTERMINATION OF HOMOSEXUALS

THE NAZI EXTERMINATION OF HOMOSEXUALS

Frank Rector

STEIN AND DAY/*Publishers*/New York

First Published in 1981

Designed by Louis A. Ditizio
Printed in the United States of America
Stein and Day/*Publishers*
Scarborough House
Briarcliff Manor, N.Y. 10510

Library of Congress Cataloging in Publication Data

Rector, Frank.
The Nazi extermination of homosexuals.

Includes index.
1. Homosexuality, Male—Germany—History.
2. Nationalsozialistische Deutsche Arbeiter-Partei
I. Title.
HQ76.2.G4R4 301.41′57′0943 79-3708
ISBN 0-8128-2729-5

To
A.R.P.
and
Charles J. Smith

Contents

Acknowledgments

1. Welcome to Germany (13)

2. The Nazi Aurora (29)

3. Dragons' Teeth (35)

4. Juggernaut (45)

5. Blood Purge (53)

6. Gay Genocide (103)

7. The Camps (127)

8. Testimony from Berlin (153)

9. Testimony from Vienna (163)

Notes (173)

Bibliography (179)

Index (183)

Photos between pages 52 & 53, 102 & 103

Acknowledgments

I am particularly grateful to Charles J. Smith, Stephen W. Foster, Warren Wyss, and James D. Steakley of the United States, and Michael J. Johnson of the United Kingdom.

I also wish to thank the United States journals *Advocate, Gay Academic Union Newsletter,* and *Gay Rights Guardian*; as well as Howard J. Erickson; Richard Ginder; Homophile Effort for Legal Protection; Hubert Kennedy; Michele Kipke; Michael A. Lombardi; William G. Niederland; Wilford H. Scott; Thomas S. Szasz; Robert Wolfe, Chief of the Captured Records Branch, National Archives, and George Wagner, National Archives Technician in the Captured Records Branch; in Austria, the Evangelical Church of the Augsburg Confession; in Canada, *Body Politic*; in Scotland, Bob Deacon; and, in the United Kingdom, David Blamires, Lionel Gibson, Anthony King, and *Gay News.*

THE NAZI EXTERMINATION OF HOMOSEXUALS

1

Welcome to Germany

The homosexual scene in Germany at the time Adolf Hitler began his climb to power in 1919 was as vibrant and virile as it was garish and gaudy. It was characterized by a gay ambiance that was merrily orgiastic, especially in Berlin, and it gave rise to the world's first organized Gay Liberation and Women's Liberation movements. There were about as many—if not more—homosexual periodicals and gay bars in Berlin in the 1920s as there now are in New York City, and Berlin of the time was abuzz with the feasibility of forming a national homosexual political party.

The sexual revolution with its free-and-easy attitudes, including wife-swapping and group sex as a moral precept, was a German "invention" of the Twenties. In wild and ugly postwar Berlin—George Grosz called it "a stone-gray corpse" of a city—an intact hymen at age 16 was grist for teasing jocularity, abortions were shrugged off, and condoms were on sale in open display in grocery stores and almost every other public mart. Nowhere was the new wave of sexual unshackling more evident than at the splendid Gartenstrasse swimming pool, where young men and women and boys and girls of all ages happily swam naked together.

Naked group bathing was one of the first expressions of Germany's blossoming libertarianism of that time to be suppressed by Hitler when he took power, even though he maintained that he was not in the least embarrassed by nudity—it was others, he said, who were: "The idea of nakedness torments only the priests, for the education they undergo makes them perverts."[1] It was a lie, of course. He had always been upset at the thought of the public display of too much skin, his own and others'; pictures and sculpture were an exception, for the most part, so long as they were not pornographic or too explicit. In private, however, he indulged a taste for erotic art and pornography, but in public he was a prude with an unctuous concern for proper conduct. He did not permit swearing or the telling of off-color jokes in his presence; gentlemen never removed their coats no matter how warm the weather; and he once was furious with Mussolini when Il Duce allowed himself to be seen in public in bathing trunks.

Hitler railed against sexual permissiveness knowing full well that sexual sermons whip up smug and self-righteous wrath, and are perennially a great mob-pleaser. He knew that sex was a good issue. The veneer of straight and gay sexual decorum had indeed disintegrated in post-World War I Germany, partly as a consequence of social and economic crises ensuing from catastrophic defeat, a product of what the Germans called their "delirium of despair." Georges Clemenceau in an earlier age referred to the condition as "the gamy peace of decadence. It will be filthy and delicious."

Despite the despair, in the heyday of the constitutional Weimar Republic, Germany was seen by many as a country of genuine modernism and freedom—sexual and otherwise. However, to many the freedom that existed was unwonted and unwanted. To some it meant freedom to starve. To others it meant having to shoulder unwelcome responsibilities for individual thought and action. Weimar freedom seemed an aimless and arid thing to many Germans because it appeared to displace traditionally strong leadership and structured social bonds. But there were also those to whom Weimar freedom meant discarding taboos in favor of an unfettered life in the midst of a sourly oppressive and grim world. T. L. Jarman observed with disapprobation: "Freedom degenerated into license; youth enjoyed the sunshine while it could. Bars for homosexuals, cafés where men danced with men, a new liberty between the sexes, nudism, camping, sun-bathing, pornographic literature in the corner kiosks—all these things were accepted as part of the new life."[2]

The sexual Mardi Gras of the era doubtless was also a result of a desperate lunge toward a reexamination and reformation of values. When a governmental system ruins lives, when it pushes its people into the gory jaws of a war of aggression, then that system is (or should be) held in question and many of its values rejected or altered. Actually, this reappraisal was launched in Switzerland during World War I. The Dada fad, for example, which originated in the Café Voltaire in Zurich among a coterie of poets, painters, and musicians, was intended to mock, deride, and spit at all the beliefs and standards of a system that had brought mankind to the bloody catastrophe of a world war.

Hitler, of course, had the simplest answer for raucous lasciviousness, for the "pleasure-lust and sexual obsession" of the period. This *terribles simplificateur* had a terribly simple answer, rationale, and solution for everything. In his Munich beer-hall cellar (*Hofbräuhaus*) speeches, the aspiring tyrant commiserated, "We dance and pursue pleasure to forget our misery." Note: He never danced with anyone, and, needless to say, his supreme pleasure pursuits were hardly life-affirming. The fillip about dancing and pursuing pleasure to meliorate misery was certainly true enough, but Hitler intended it as a sop to the mob. The real and simple reason, he roared, for all the pleasure-lust and sexual obsession lay at the fonts of moral turpitude—the Weimar Republic and the Jews. He screamed that the Republic and Jews were behind a despicable *vergnügungswut,* the madness for pleasure. In explosive speech after speech he hammered on the theme of moral laxity and those he said had fostered it.

"It is no accident," Hitler shouted in Munich tirades, "that more and more kinds of diversion [read "perversions"] are constantly being invented." The Jews were deliberately engineering moral decay because, exclaimed Hitler, they are the enemy of *völkisch* values and morals. Stabbing and slashing the air with phallic gestures, he would repeat over and over that the Jew "destroys . . . national pride, which is the strength of a nation, with mockery and shameless training in vice," a statement that made its original appearance in his first political tract, dated September 16, 1919.[3] He thundered that Germany was turning into a "hothouse of sexual imagery and stimulation," which was threatening to engulf the whole culture in "the suffocating perfume of modern eroticism."[4] This from a man who reportedly liked his girl friends to squat over him and urinate and defecate in his face.[5]

Cascades of cheers greeted Hitler's common brand of morality and anti-Semitism because the mass of gentile straight Germans did blame Jews for the spread of sexual shoddiness and voluptuousness, general profligacy, and misery: "If the relaxation of censorship in the Weimar era led to the publication of lesbian and homosexual magazines, and discussion and literature on all aspects of sex and the human psyche proliferated; if there was an economically conditioned increase in the incidence of abortion and the number of juvenile prostitutes (male as well as female); if some advanced schools included sex-education in their curriculum and had pupil committees . . . it was tempting to echo Treitschke's phrase, 'The Jews are our misfortune.' The Judeodemocracy was blamed for the twenties' cult of the new, the meretricious and the sensational. . . . Yet the main charge against the Jews was that they dominated such spheres as banking, business, real estate, brokerage, moneylending and cattle-trading," says Richard Grunberger in *The 12-Year Reich*.[6]

This latter seeming dominion of the Jews probably upset most Germans more than anything else. In an oversimplification of anti-Semitism, the German historian Friedrich Meinecke says in *The German Catastrophe*, "Among those who drank too hastily and greedily of the cup of power which had come to them were many Jews. They appeared in the eyes of persons with anti-Semitic feeling to be the beneficiaries of the German defeat and revolution. Everyone else in Germany, aside from these beneficiaries, seemed irrevocably consigned to misery."[7] This state of affairs was readily visible in Berlin, which is surely one of the principal reasons why Hitler was so violently "choked with disgust" over the "moral depravity" in that city. This combined with the fact that sophisticated, cosmopolitan Weimar Berlin was, for the time being, largely indifferent to the raging antics of an upstart politician from southern Germany.

Hitler's moral hypocrisy is understandable only if we stop to consider the nature of hypocrites. They, like Hitler, often devoutly believe what they say; quite frequently there is no questioning the single-minded sincerity of their statements. But if the rock of their self-righteousness is turned over, what will be found beneath is likely to be shocking. Robert G. L. Waite revealed in his *The Psychopathic God* that according to the Führer's one-time court jester and personal piano player, Ernst Hanfstaengl, underneath Hitler's ostentatious, loud-mouthed, phony morality was a mind inordinately excited by rape, prostitution, syphilis, and "the most disgusting" sexual practices. He wanted to look at sex. He was infatuated with von Stuck's sensuous paintings; he had a library of pornography; he had blue films made especially for his private viewing; and he drew pictures which "only a perverted voyeur could have committed to paper."[8]

Hitler's *joie de vivre* seems to have been "depraved" sexual practices, mostly of the heterosexual variety. (Among his other favorite topics of conversation was to describe in gruesome detail the torture techniques used by the Gestapo.) August Kubizek says in his book, *Young Hitler: The Story of Our Friendship,* that Hitler was particularly interested in deviate sexual behavior and chattered by the hour about it.

Though Hitler's thoughts were awash in sex and whatever may be considered its perversions, he was afraid of genital sex acts in any form, and employed the same psychological defenses against perversion that he used against feelings of latent homosexuality and fears of Jewishness: denial, projection, and punishment. His immediate reaction on seeing photographs depicting "gross types of deviate sexual activity" was that the males involved could not possibly be Germans, that they must be of Jewish extraction. Whether or not Hitler intended that remark as a kind of race joke, he knew very well that gentile Germans were fully capable of such "gross types of deviate sexual activity."

Hitler detested Berlin not so much for its "gross moral depravities" but because Berlin was so *open* about matters sexual and seemed to foster democratic liberalism and pluralism; and because, as mentioned, of all the major cities in Germany it was at first one of the least receptive to Hitler in his ascent to power. He referred shrilly to Berlin as that "great Babylonian whore," but he was not the only one to have this view. Richard Hanser called the city "an enormous sexual circus" and reports that another writer, the homosexual Klaus Mann, said: " 'Look at me!' the German capital trumpets, boastful even in its desperation. 'I am Babylon, the monster among cities. Sodom and Gomorrah together were not half so degenerate, not half so horrible as I am! Step right up, ladies and gentlemen, with me anything goes and no holds barred! The night life of Berlin—man alive, the world has never seen anything like it! Vices you never even heard of! Once we had an unsurpassed army; now we have unsurpassed perversities! A tremendous selection! There's something doing here, believe me! Don't miss it!' "[9]

There is probably something doing everywhere. Almost no city or hamlet on earth is without its so-called seamy side, although seamy can be a matter of personal definition. Still, there is no gainsaying Hitler and his opinion that Berlin and other parts of Germany had markedly and stridently become hothouses of sexual imagery and stimulation. German cabarets, bars, beer halls, and dance halls throbbed to the pulsing beat of jazz, ragtime, and husky, throaty torch songs. There was music, laughter, and frank, open homosexual desire, which was hardly ever coy and seldom limp-wristed, except among male transvestites and effeminate gays.

Tourists the world over tramped to Berlin to soak up some sin, made all the more delightfully wicked when illuminated in the romantic flickering glow of gas lights. There were whorehouses galore—for everyone—for straights and gays and every shade in between. Pregnant prostitutes were in popular demand, and while wending one's way along Berlin's Kurfürstendamm or Friedrichstrasse, skirting pimps, dope peddlers, and the stumps of war-mutilated veterans reduced to beggary—who would sell their Iron Crosses (or themselves) for the price of a piece of sausage—one could if one were so disposed pursue little girls of 10 and 11, rouged and wearing short baby dresses, who promenaded from midnight to dawn in competition with lush blondes swathed in furs. There was also dartingly peripatetic sex-for-sale competition from doll-like little boys wearing lipstick, powder, and eye shadow who hawked and plied their mouths, buttocks, and caresses in alleyways and side streets.

Sex-for-sale and sex-for-the-sake-of-sex prowling were not just a murky nighttime affair. The homosexual traffic began at about 9 A.M., and "almost any street in Central Berlin had its sprinkling of *Stundenhotels* or *Absteige*—small discreet hotels or private flats where a room could be used for an hour or less. An astonishing number of seemingly respectable spinsters and widows, and of dignified elderly men who before inflation might have been living on dividends, let their spare rooms for this purpose . . . [and had] a working arrangement with a . . . string of boys who thus knew where to take their transient clients," writes Michael Davidson in *The World, the Flesh and Myself.*[10]

In short, post-World War I Berlin was not merely one of Europe's most notorious fleshpots. It was seen as the best of worlds and the worst of worlds, where cultural life was the most creative in Germany's history, where creativity in all fields of human endeavor was simply astounding, but did little to advance political freedom or democratic institutions.

Michael Davidson, whose autobiographical life history of a lover of boys, *The World, the Flesh and Myself,* is a homophile classic, said he "loathed Berlin for the first week; and then suddenly . . . I saw that it was the most exciting town one could conceive of: Babylon, Gomorrah, Rome in decay; and yet galvanic with an intellectual liveliness. . . . On the one hand, all the *boue* that one nostalgic for it could desire—squalor, drunkenness, penury, an ubiquitous underworld, dramatic violence and despair, the turbulence of gangster politics, the whole spectrum of sexual lust, with some unimagined hues added, displayed like fruit in an open Mediterranean market-place; on the other, a novel flowering—as if rain had fallen after a long drought—of architecture, the theatre, music, satire—a new liberty of ideas, a wonderful release of the individual. Of course, within five years all this exploring spirit was crushed—less, perhaps, by Hitler than by its own libertarian blindness which allowed Hitler to pinion it from behind."[11] However much, according to Plato, that tyranny may grow out of democracy, Frederick B. Artz said in 1941 in his book *1917 and 1941*: "Freedom, justice, tolerance, and decency have never struck deep roots in the German political tradition. In that sense Germany has not been . . . a normal, civilized country, and to deal with it as though it were is to act on a profound and dangerous illusion."

When Hitler became top wolf, among the first to feel his fury were the homosexual organizations and publications. The Nazi Party's Program, signed by Hitler in Munich on February 24, 1920, as explicated by Gottfried Feder, called for the suppression of all printed matter that "offends the dignity of the German people." Before Hitler's ascendancy, however, pre-totalitarian Germany, notably Berlin, showed, at least superficially, liberal toleration for homosexuals.

For example, Davidson tells about being accosted in Berlin by a young hustler who was being offensive. A policeman, unaware that Davidson was trying to shake off the lad, approached and kindly advised: "You should be very careful about what boys you pick up—there are some bad ones about." The tolerance in Berlin of the Twenties extended in some cases to the fathers of gays. Davidson recalls how a friend of his once found himself confronted on his doorstep by a well-dressed gentleman inquiring after his son: " 'I believe you're a friend of a boy named ———?'. Davidson's friend ——— was taken aback; but the visitor hastened to put him at his ease. 'Oh, it's all right,' he said. 'I just came to call—I always like to know what sort of man my son is going with.' "[12]

In this kaleidoscope of erotica, straights flocked to gawk and giggle at the queers and queens in Berlin's Mikado on Krausenstrasse, where male prostitutes (about 2,000 in Berlin alone—all neatly listed in a police card-index file) cavorted with transvestites and gays of every type and variety. Male transvestites at the Mikado and elsewhere punctiliously used the lavatory marked *Damen,* and lesbians in men's suits, shoes, shirts, ties, and hats used the *Herren* toilet. Considering that other clientele adhered to the normal division of usage, and that transvestites are not ipso facto homosexual, there was quite a bit of cozy togetherness and not a few hilarious scenes in the toilets.

The Mikado was one of about forty gay bars in Berlin, which were frequented by a number of leading government and industry officials who regularly went to certain bars to pick up drunken sailors. Some of the bars were raunchy, for the gay type who likes lots of macho with his sex, while the lesbian bars were usually very chic. Many male gay bars and cabarets were snootily equivocal, and you really could not tell where you were until someone wryly observed, "What do here all deese handsome young men?"—along with paunchy, pudgy, pompaded, jowly business types, very correct civil servants, and primly proper military officers. It was a George Grosz scene come to life.

Most gay hangouts were urbane, civil, sophisticated. Ben Hecht remembered a "group of homosexual aviators, who were not unique in the Berlin of the time—'elegant fellows, perfumed and monocled and usually full of heroin or cocaine. They made love to one another, openly kissing in the cafe booths. . . .' "[13] And, Davidson says, "There were dozens of places like the *Nüremberger Diele* and *Kantdiele,* where middleaged stockbrokers danced with elegant pansies. But we enjoyed the more specialized resorts like the *Schnurbart Diele,* as it was nicknamed—the 'moustache cafe'—where men with magnificent moustaches went to meet other men with moustaches. 'I've got a bigger one than yours,' one would say to a new acquaintance—meaning, at any rate in the first place, his moustache."[14]

Various other attractions were the cabarets featuring crossdress dances, where all the men dressed as women and all the women dressed as men whether or not they were transvestites, and a gay bar that plump, elderly men bellied-up to attired in little short knickers or sailor suits. If some found all this amusing but too tame, there were places publicly catering to nearly every so-called perversion and fetish for which one might have a taste. One could whip or be whipped; be inundated with bodily wastes; be fellated while being strangled at the individual's own behest to within an inch of death. There were places where teenage males looking for a mother substitute could bed a matronly woman, whose life had likely been shattered by the war and to whom prostitution had become one of the few diminishing means of survival; and where fatherly gentlemen could readily hire 10-year-old playmates, female or male or a mixture of both.

Berlin unashamedly and deservedly earned the sobriquet of Sin

City. The capital and much of Germany had indeed become a sexual circus, which as often as not was as sad as it was gay. Davidson says, "... the place I liked best—because, I suppose, it was so touching, and tore at my mother's heart—was the 'Adonis-Diele,' where farouche yearning boys slumped for hours at the tables, [with] long yellow hair falling into their eyes and their most urgent desire a pull at a cigarette. Each time the curtains at the door were pushed apart, all eyes would turn to the new customer, each face hungry to be chosen—to be given a cigarette, some beer and *Bockwurst* and, later, a bed to sleep in. These weren't professionally 'on the game'—they would have been elsewhere had they been that; they were just unhappy, homeless boys."[15]

That particular aspect of the homosexual milieu was surely the same as it was and is in every metropolis in the world at any time in history, though the scene described, and many like it, were doubtless more uncommonly widespread throughout Germany because of the shattered postwar economic situation. Perhaps this may to some extent account for why Germany was widely seen as "the most homosexual nation on earth." Closer to the truth is that so many German males were more bisexually active. (Germany's renowned youth movement was a pronounced homosexual influence; this will be discussed in later pages.)

Gays generally did not recruit boys or men into homosexual behavior any more than a flesh hustler today is seduced into gay sex. Many a gay-hunting hustler peddles his favors for money on Friday so that he can treat his girl friend to a high-style weekend of lovemaking. However, practice frequently evolves its logical course after a time and, in many cases, straight males develop a liking for gay pleasures; or, as the old cliché has it, "Today's trade is tomorrow's competition." Many of the boys and young men of post-World War I Germany were not *homo*sexual, they were simply *sexual.* They might or might not have had a true tolerance for sexual diversity but they were accommodating because the real world, particularly when times are bad, has a way of impressing its own realities upon those who have no vested interest in living in a world of delusion.

But along came Hitler who knew better than most that, conversely, dark times can also evilly brew a vested interest in delusion.

Many of those same farouche yearning boys with long yellow hair, along with their gay lovers, would soon clip their hair to a brush-cut and don brown and black shirts and the red-white-and-black swastika because the genius Hitler insidiously created, *precisely* and *deliberately,* a vested interest in delusion. He exploited the irrational side of human nature, both in himself and others, with shrewd calculation; then his followers themselves completed the conversion: ". . . they imposed upon political events unreal, phantasmagoric imaginings, fantasies out of detective stories or spy thrillers," said ex-Nazi Albert Krebs in his memoirs.[16]

That may help explain why there were such large numbers of gays and bisexuals in the Nazi Movement at the beginning and during the halcyon years before the purge of homosexuals began. To state it simply, *oversimply,* in a psychological sense they had nowhere else to go. Moreover, as Hitler intended, the masculine vigor, adventure, thrust, vitality, and virile camaraderie of the Party were to many gays an irresistible attraction, just as it was for heterosexual males.

There is no question, surely, that Hitler realized how utterly and supremely effectively he could utilize (and brutalize) young male homosexuals for his purposes. He surreptitiously welcomed them into his Party with open arms—figuratively, that is. He was neither a homosexual nor a bisexual; he had no interest at all in having sex with another male, and, insofar as is known, never did have such contact. (For that matter, he had little interest in having sex with females, either—yet, he was a sexually obsessed man. This is by no means the first of complex contradictions we shall encounter in Hitler.) Nevertheless, in his early political career that began in 1919, when he was 30 years old, he ran in the company of some pretty powerful homosexuals, among whom was Ernst Röhm, who became Chief of the SA (Storm Troopers). There was gossip that he and Hitler had a bit of a fling. This resulted in speculation at the time, and since, that in the early days the then quite good-looking Adolf Hitler made ends meet and secured key support for his infant Party by granting sexual favors to influential gays. This possibility, however, is too remote to be seriously considered.[17]

Hitler had a pathological fear and hatred of capitulation in every sense of the word, in any way whatever. Above all, he was in fact homophobic. Still, Hitler was not stupid. From his point of view he quite intelligently put aside his homophobia and soft-pedalled *that* issue when he saw how the muscularity of homosexuals could strengthen his fledgling Party. This political realism had nothing at all to do with Hitler's contradictory feeling that gays were *basically* degenerate and feminine. Hitler was so deeply divided that he often was torn between opposing qualities: omnipotent and vulnerable, sophisticated and savage, creative and destructive, pragmatic and fanatical, brave and cowardly, lethargic and industrious, rigid and malleable, pathetic and masterful, cruel and kind. One idly speculates whether he would have shelved his hatred of Jews in his self-interest if anti-Semitism had not been convenient and predictably successful an issue in Germany. After all, he did make his favorite cook, who was of Jewish descent, an "Honorary Aryan," and the Number 2 Nazi, Hermann Göring, had a virtual stable of "pet Jews." He once proclaimed, "A Jew is what I say a Jew is." As for Röhm, he privately laughed at the obsessive anti-Semitism of the Movement and tolerated it merely as a propaganda device.

Homophobic though Hitler was, the Program of the National Socialist German Workers Party contains no specific reference to homosexuality or homosexuals. Gottfried Feder, one of the godfathers of Nazism, appointed by Hitler as "final arbiter" (Hitler was, of course, *the* final arbiter) of all questions touching the Program, had nothing to say about homosexuals in his 1927 book enucleating the Program's 25 Points.[18] Hitler's homophobia did not surface until 1933-1934, when gays had come to affect adversely his New Order designs—out of which grew the simple solution of murdering them en masse. Yet, it should be noted that, in the 1934 Blood Purge, Röhm and friends were not ordered executed by Hitler solely because they were gay—although that was one of the principal reasons touted at the time—but because they were rocking Hitler's ship of state and the foundations of his master power plans. A macabre joke that circulated underground after the Blood Purge carnage was: "Lieber Gott! If Hitler killed Röhm because our Leader just found out about Röhm's homosexuality, I fear to wonder what Der Führer will do when he finds out about Dr. Goebbels' club foot!"

The persecution of homosexuals simply because they were homosexuals began *officially* when Hitler became Chancellor in 1933, but did not become a "Final Solution" until the Röhm Purge. For simplicity's sake, gay genocide is dated as beginning with the June 30, 1934, Blood Purge (or the Night of the Long Knives, as it was also known), because in effect that was the starting point. In reality, the persecution of gays bubbled and boiled for years before 1934. It broke into dramatic conflagration with the Nazis' burning of the holdings in Magnus Hirschfeld's Institute of Sexual Science in Berlin in 1933. Hirschfeld's institute was primarily homosexually oriented. Along with condemned holdings in other libraries, this was the first Nazi book-burning party, and a symbolic auto-da-fé of homosexuals, although most Nazi gays probably did not then know it or admit it.

Hirschfeld—a Jew, transvestite, and effeminate homosexual—helped launch in Berlin on May 15, 1897, the world's first homosexual emancipation organization, the Scientific Humanitarian Committee. Inasmuch as Hirschfeld was a Jew, his institute's position anything but pro-Nazi, his reform efforts on behalf of gays disparaged by many homosexuals themselves (they could not stomach his transvestism, his effeminacy, his deplorable inability to keep his mouth shut, and, for many, his Judaism itself), the attack against him and his institute was seen as an anti-Semitic act rather than as an expression of anti-homosexual sentiment by gays in and out of the Nazi Movement. Much of the public, however, correctly read it as an attack against both Judaism and homosexuality. Straight Nazis referred to the institute as a Jewish breeding ground of homosexual dirt and filth.

The persecution at the least, and the destruction at the worst, of homosexuals was almost inevitable because of the nature of the mentality of heterosexual Fascists, who could not for long or at all tolerate gays. In the beginning, homosexuals were useful to the Nazi Movement and greatly contributed to its driving force. That staved off for a while hysterical homophobia witch hunts. A more-or-less accurate assessment of how gaydom stood in the scheme of things is given by Davidson: There are those, says Davidson, "who believe that Hitlerism was a stern reaction to this 'German decadence' [homosexuality], or alternatively regard the Nazi Party itself as a foul edifice of degeneracy—in either case blaming Germany's blatant homosexuality for the Hitler tyranny. But both assumptions are false. Hitler didn't, morally, care tuppence about homosexuality [*sic*]; in the early years of his power he tried, so to speak, to cover it over with a clean cloth just as he tried to deny poverty by pushing its more public signs, like beggars and street musicians, out of public sight. But politically he used homosexuality, like anything else, wherever it fitted expediency. Ernst Röhm wasn't shot because the Nazi Party felt outraged by the abrupt discovery that he was 'having' his Storm Troopers—that had been known for ages; but because his sway over the S.A. had become a menace to Hitler. In the Hitler Youth the 'dear love of comrades' was evilly turned to a political end. [Davidson alludes to the fact that many SA men came from the ranks of the Hitler Youth and brought their dear love of comrades with them.] And if the Nazi hierarchy was well larded with homosexuals, so was Wilhelm II's court and so was the Weimar Republic. The 'German decadence' wasn't a national trauma left like a scar by 1918 [the end of World War I]; and it wasn't, I suppose, the invention of Frederick the Great and Voltaire. If it's a decadence, it's been decaying for a very long time."[19]

On the one hand, Hitler overlooked homosexuality (see Waite's *The Psychopathic God* for a discussion of Hitler's duality); on the other, he hated homosexuals as he hated so much else in life. Hitler's homophobia was probably rooted in his fears about his own concept of masculinity. He was determined that no one would ever suspect him of sexual inadequacy, femininity, or homosexuality. Foreign correspondent H. R. Knickerbocker, who was on the scene, once said about Hitler (they knew each other and loathed one another; Knickerbocker was lucky he left Germany before Hitler got around to killing him): "There is something absurd even about his stance as he rides his victorious chariot [mammoth Mercedes-Benz autos] through freshly conquered [German] cities. He is softly fat about the hips and this gives his figure a curiously female appearance. A scientist friend of mine watching him once remarked that Hitler seemed afflicted by *steatopygia* [original italics], which he defined as 'an excessive development of fat on the buttocks, especially in *females* [original italics].' It is possible that the strongly feminine element in Hitler's character is one of the reasons for his violence. He realizes his femininity, is ashamed of it, wishes to be a man, and overcompensates by brutal behavior. This little fatty-hipped, slope-shouldered, lonely figure, standing so inflexibly, his arm outstretched so tautly, his eyes staring over the heads of his subjects, is incredible. 'No,' you say to yourself, 'this can't be true.' "[20] Whatever its genesis, Hitler's infatuation with hardness and brutality became a normative value in the Third Reich.

The quintessence of Hitler was that he had an implacable hatred for every human being on earth not willing or suitable to help him place Deutschland in command of the world with himself the globe's supreme ruler. Hitler did not hold homosexuals suitable for that purpose, but they *were* willing. So, suitable or not, for the time being, Hitler used homosexuals. For the time being, he turned his homophobia down to a simmer and placed it on a back-burner. Not until later would it burst into a "fiery sea of devouring flames," to use Hitler's own expression.

2

The Nazi Aurora

Sociologist Zevedei Barbu says it is hard to maintain that the Nazi Movement had a distinct class character. All strata of the German nation contributed to the Nazi triumph. Barbu explains that the *classless* element rather than a particular social class should first be considered in order to understand Nazism. The structure of the Movement represented the entire nation. World War I, inflation, and depression had left vast numbers of Germans classless, or feeling classless, as well as scarred by bitterness. They loathed the Weimar Republic, which they held responsible for the postwar "delirium of despair." Hitler made his appeal to people who felt themselves ignored or slighted by the established parties—"To those," he said, "who are suffering and tormented, those without peace, the unhappy and discontented."[1]

The Nazi Movement became a common meeting ground for most individuals and groups with a deprived or ruined social status because this is what Hitler intended from the beginning. "In order to activate these millions of nameless people he must [and did] offer them a grand design, a framework in which the individual could seek his own place, an ideal nebulous enough to fulfill all expectations," says Hans Peter Bleuel in *Sex and Society in Nazi Ger-*

many.[2] He imbued the Movement with mass appeal among most of the dispossessed, a condition that applied to Germans from aristocrats on down to the bottom of the social heap, where Hitler was to be found. He spoke for many déclassés, notable among whom were homosexuals in the deceptively liberated Weimar Republic. This in part explains why so many gays were attracted to Hitler's siren song.

Gays mistakenly believed that at last they, along with Hitler himself and multitudes of other déclassés, had found something to which they could belong and with which they could mold a Brave New World. Hitler did not straightforwardly disabuse gays of this notion until much later, not until his takeover of power had been carried out in the main by declassed individuals. The Nazis "recruited their members from a cross section of Germans, and Nazism both reflected and responded to their desires. Hitler succeeded not because of a conspiracy of the few but because his movement gave high hope to the many of solving the pressing psychological demands of a people living under conditions of acute stress. Defeated by war and broken by inflation, the uprooted, humiliated, and insecure Germans were attracted to Nazism because they felt that their personal problems would be solved by a movement that promised to supply everything they lacked as individuals: dramatic action, a sense of purpose, a feeling of power," says Robert G. L. Waite in *Hitler and Nazi Germany.*[3]

Countless gays believed Hitler when he said: "We are determined to create a new community out of the German peoples—a community formed of men of every status and profession and of every so-called class. . . . All classes must be welded together into a single German nation. . . . You could look upon me as the man who belongs to no class, who belongs to no group, who is above all such considerations. . . . To me everyone is entirely equal. . . . Only when the entire German people becomes a single community of sacrifice can we hope and expect that Providence will stand by us in the future."[4]

While it is true that the composition of the Party and the Movement included all levels of the social pyramid, its brains and brawn and dynamism came from youthful middle-to-lower white-collar and blue-collar masses and hordes of unemployed youths. *The spearhead of the Nazi Movement was Youth.* The sham-idealistic attraction of the chimera of the national community (*Volksgemeinschaft*) cast a spell on the young. No one knows and no one will ever know what percentages of that Nazi vanguard and rank-and-file were gay, bisexual, or heterosexual. Some historians believe homosexuals were *the* center of the Nazi Movement. All we know at present is that "many" homosexuals were in the Party. By rough Kinseyan reckoning, perhaps they constituted 10 to 13 percent of the membership. This is admittedly a flimsy extrapolation, but anything else would be even purer guesswork. Published German estimates of the number of gays in 1919-1933 Germany seem highly dubious because they are very low. It took an Alfred C. Kinsey to determine what the real homosexual percentage is likely to be in any modern society.

Whatever their number, many of those gays were monsters. Hitler often got precisely what he desired: "I want vigorous, commanding, and cruel young men with the strength and beauty of young beasts of prey . . . [and without a] conscience. . . . [That is a] Jewish invention; like circumcision it mutilates man."[5] Most of them knew what they were doing, morally, from the very start, and positively reveled in it. In musing about the Nazis, Fascism, and mankind, psychiatrist Carl G. Jung said in October 1938: "Not everybody has virtues, but everybody has the low animal instincts, the basic primitive caveman suggestibility, the suspicious and vicious traits of the savage. The result is that when you get a nation of many millions of people, it is not even human. It is a lizard or a crocodile or a wolf. Its statesmen cannot have a higher morality than the animal-like mass morality of the nation, although individual statesmen of the democratic states may attempt to behave a little better."[6]

The spirit and aura of Nazism as we most commonly perceive it cannot be credited to Hitler alone. In 1919, at about the time Hitler was taking his first faltering political steps, the German poet Walther Mehring published a prophetic Dada rhyme satirizing the savage mentality of Germany's post-World War I Free Corps (Free Corpsmen, mostly young veterans and assorted fanatics, formed the main body of Hitler's Storm Troopers, the SA*):

---

*Thus abbreviation derives from the German *Sturmabteilung*.

C'mon, boys, let's all go
Off to the pogrom with a ho-ho-ho
Pull in your bellies and throw out the Jews
With swastika and poison gas
Let's have a go at murder in the mass.[7]

Hitler synthesized Nazism—he did not invent it. But, wherever the spider's web of Nazism stretched, Hitler wove it and occupied its dead center. He was the author of the Movement, he knew what and whom to use, to discard, and how to put it all together and make it *work*.

"Hitler . . . was a consummate actor, with the actor's and orator's facility for absorbing himself in a role and convincing himself of the truth of what he was saying at the time he said it. In his early years he was often awkward and unconvincing, but with practice the part became second nature to him, and with the immense prestige of success behind him, and the resources of a powerful state at his command, there were few who could resist the impression of the piercing eyes, the Napoleonic pose, and the 'historic' personality," says Waite in *Hitler and Nazi Germany*.[8] All of these Hitler painstakingly practiced for countless hours before a full-length mirror. He did the same in private before the camera of his personal photographer, Heinrich Hoffmann. Hitler used the photos to study his every gesture, stance, and facial expression so that he could improve his performance. To further perfect his style, he studied popular Munich comedian Weiss Ferdl's tricks for holding the attention of a crowd despite the racket and bustle of a room full of uninhibited drinkers. Hitler also took lessons in delivery and gesture from a prominent actor.

H. R. Knickerbocker, who knew Hitler well ("I had a series of interviews with him, and was present at many of the great moments of his career"), says in *Is Tomorrow Hitler's?*: "Indeed Hitler is, more than anything else, an actor. He will go on being one for the rest of his life, a great actor who in his role as tyrant conqueror will have affected the destinies of more millions of people than any other human being in history, but an actor to the last. . . ."[9] Hitler himself once said he was the greatest actor in Europe. He played the role of Führer with such megalomaniacal conviction that it became his undoing because he eventually took his self-assumed omniscience not as playacting but as a fact. Waite concludes: "Hitler never actually possessed the personal strength, integrity, and purpose that he projected. But he gave the illusion of possessing them. And that was sufficient. He moved men because he was able—in Heiden's phrase—'to act out greatness,' to change himself from a hesitant and unsure little man to a person of towering historic force who paralyzed opposition and commanded millions to do his will."[10]

"Adolf Hitler *is* the Party! The Party *is* Adolf Hitler!" shouted Rudolf Hess at the Nuremberg rally in 1934. Pulitzer-prize-winning Knickerbocker reported at the time of Der Führer's rise: "Hitler is the whole regime, its author, its parent, its spirit, its brains, and its boss."[11] Waite says, "He was not the interpreter of an ideology; he was the Idea made incarnate. *He was Nazism.* He and he alone was the ultimate arbiter of all matters political, social, aesthetic, cultural, moral. His whim, quite literally, became the law of the land."[12] *Ein Volk! Ein Reich! Ein Führer! Sieg Heil!*

Never in modern history has one man's personality so completely dominated and controlled a society. This means, regardless of what many writers claim, homosexuals did *not* set the tone or exemplify the moral filth of Hitler's Movement any more than did heterosexuals. Homosexuals were a significant element in the success and stench of the Movement, but not nearly to the extent that has widely been attributed to them. Hitler was the spellbinder who fulfilled the prophecy of his fellow Austrian, the poet Hofmannsthal: "Politics is magic. He who knows how to summon the forces of the deep, him people will follow."[13]

Hitler indeed spoke to the forces of the deep, appealing to both gays and gay-haters. However, the mistake the myopic so often make is in not grasping that Hitler was fundamentally and hysterically anti-homosexual. He equated homosexuality with femininity, and femininity with capitulation, the surrendering of one's will to another, and he would rather die than do that, which is exactly what he ultimately did do. Though there was plentiful evidence to the contrary that should have made plain to him the hairy masculine macho of German gays, Hitler's stereotyped image perceived them as womanlike, surrendering, and therefore essentially weak—

traits Hitler despised. He would "'never surrender as a woman surrenders to a man'"—"'Never! Never!'"[14]

Hitler's homophobia, though extreme, was subject to being contained or overridden for a time by his political first-things-first drive to power. His attitude was not untypical, and homophobia was not, needless to say, peculiar to Hitler and straight Nazis. Virtually every government on earth today discriminates against or persecutes its homosexual minority to some extent. As such, the degree of anti-homosexual virulence can be an indicator of how far institutions and individuals are veering toward inhumanity.

In that gays without number rushed wildly into the Nazi fold, only later to wind up dancing at the end of a rope, merely illustrates that gays can be as stupid as anyone else (and as immoral). Open homosexuality and Fascism are not compatible, at least not for very long. One or the other must eventually go. In the end, it turned out that déclassé homosexuals had nowhere to go but up the chimney.

3

Dragons' Teeth

"At the moment of writing it is only eight hours since I watched a Hitler demonstration in the German capital, with an emotional people in the throes of what appeared to me a fanatical, abnormal condition. In this demonstration hundreds of thousands took the strange Hitler oath that would bind them, so they believed, forever to der Führer and the Hakenkreuz [swastika]. When the last word of the Leader had died down and the band had started the Deutschland song, very softly at first and then stronger, its swelling tunes being carried on the winds of the trees of the Brandenburger Thor and Unter den Linden, I beheld a people aroused to an orgy of emotion. . . . When the music stopped and the last tunes were carried away over the thousands and thousands who stood at attention, the Leader spoke again—'And now we are coming to the oath, which repeat with me. *'I swear to be true to Adolf Hitler, our Führer, and swear obedience.'* Then all took the oath in absolute solemnity."[1] This scene in the dawning Armageddon was sketched by Hendrik de Leeuw in his *Sinful Cities of the Western World.*

That was the culmination of the New Order dream after Hitler "seized" power in 1933 (actually, it was handed to him, first when he was appointed Chancellor and later when the Enabling Act was passed that granted him dictatorial powers). The dream began in the 1890s with the germination of Germany's youth movement, which occurred innocently enough when Herman Hoffmann, a Berlin student, formed a study group for shorthand. Occasionally, the youths went hiking into the countryside on weekends.

Hoffmann's sexual orientation is not known, but he apparently was something of an intellectual who rebelled against the strictures of bourgeois society. He was "convinced that the individual, instead of passively surrendering to the impersonal and atomizing forces of industrialism, should actively control them. And in order to do this he had to be made aware of his natural environment in the first place. Youth had to rediscover nature, the fields, woods, brooks, lakes, and meadows from which the city dweller had been alienated. Nature, Hoffmann felt, had to be experienced in the raw: the burning scorch of the sun, the whiplash of the rainstorm and the snowstorm. . . . A haystack was preferable any time to a well-made bed, fresh air to nicotine, and water to alcohol. . . . In order to be free one had to break the existing conventions; in place of the prevailing greeting of a simultaneous bow and clicking of heels, Hoffmann thought it sufficient to raise one's right arm in the ancient form of salute, accompanied by a 'Heil!' " says H. W. Koch in *The Hitler Youth.*[2]

A close friend of Hoffmann's, a schoolteacher named Karl Fischer, got the German youth movement off the ground because he was a charismatic leader (his pupils Heiled! him and called him Der Führer). Due to him, the movement assumed shape, identity, and a program, and came to be known as the *Wandervögel* (Birds of Passage, or Wandering Birds), formally named as such in 1901. The term *Wandervögel* had been taken from a tombstone inscription, which, sadly, was portentously apt. The *Wandervögel*—and all the numerous youth splinter organizations (except the ones for Communist and Jewish youths)—were destined to be pressed into the Hitler Youth, and thence to the SA, SS,* the Armed Forces, and other formations.

---

*These initials are derived from the German *Schutzstaffel,* meaning "Defense Echelon."

The youth movement revived German folklore, folksongs, and folkdancing, and nudism was adopted by some groups. Macho dark shirts, shorts, and hobnailed boots were de rigueur for the young males, and girls, who formed their own *Wandervögel* groups, adapted a simple and tasteful Bavarian women's folk costume as their uniform. The new *Jugendkultur* (youth culture) was very *völkisch,* and that is partly what was wrong with it. Jewish youths, for instance, were generally barred from membership; they formed their own organizations. Waite says the youth movement "encouraged belief in mystical nationalism, expectations of a new and racially pure [togetherness of] *Volksgemeinschaft* [which, gays believed, would include homosexuals], and faith in the coming of a powerful political Führer."[3] Thus the seemingly innocent youth movement unwittingly sowed the teeth of dragons.

James H. McRandle says in *The Track of the Wolf* that the "movement was spontaneous, translating sentiment directly into action, with thought as a kind of intermittent and subordinate guide."[4] Waite says that sizeable elements of the movement both before and after World War I "emphasized the mystic fellowship of the *Volk,* as opposed to the rights of the individual. An incessant refrain throughout the literature of the movement was one that would be later taken up by Hitler's propaganda machine: The individual is nothing; the *Volk* is everything. This emphasis on the *Volksgemeinschaft* inevitably led to an attack on the democratic processes which were struggling for expression in Imperial Germany. It also led to racism. . . . The young people who longed for a new *Volksgemeinschaft* were not very specific about the term, but a few things were clear. This 'New Order' would not be liberal-democratic, nor would it be Marxist. Rather, it would be a kind of German national socialism. Only a mighty Führer could bring all Germans together into this 'racial community of true socialism'; Jews were not wanted. . . . Of all the words that echoed with mysterious meaning around the campfires, the most compelling" were *Volk* and *Reich* and *Führer.*[5]

Perhaps the German youth movement might have come to a better end if the Kaiser and later the Weimar Republic had taken youth seriously. Although government, army, and the churches recognized the importance of attracting youth into their ranks, most of the established political parties did not.[6]

Hitler made no such mistake. He welcomed youth, but the idea of harnessing under-18-year-olds did not originate with him but with a 17-year-old, Gustav Adolf Lenk. Lenk's application to join the SA was rejected because 18 was the minimum age. So, Lenk proposed that a Nazi youth organization be formed for 10- to 17-year-olds. Hitler heartily approved the young man's proposal and issued an order on February 25, 1922, calling for what was to become known, on March 18, 1922, as the Youth League of the National Socialist Workers Party (the Hitler Youth—Hitler *Jugend*—was not so named until 1933). This led the German youth movement straight into the trap set by the aggressive irrationalism of Nazi ideologies. The SA was given charge of the youth formation, which it at first resented, saying it did not want to be nursemaid to a bunch of kids.

The indifference to youth shown by politicians other than Hitler owed much to the fact that the youth movement's leaders preferred to give vent to feelings of discontent, particularly discontent about the older generation. "Negation rather than affirmation, elusion rather than conclusion, were the characteristic marks of those who in the age-group between twelve and nineteen formed the main body of the Youth Movement. From the lack of a clearly-formulated program the step into irrationalism was very often all too easily taken," says Koch.[7]

By incorporating youth into the Nazi Movement, the Party flattered them by in effect treating them as adults. This encouraged the adolescents' natural tendency to resist parental authority, and the net result was that the Nazi Revolution was bidding for the allegiance of the children over the heads of their parents. The Nazis' intention, once they realized the political value of Lenk's plan, was to isolate youth completely from the influence of teachers, parents, and clergymen, and in this way to get a complete hold over it.

An inevitable consequence of the German youth movement, aside from political considerations, was the confrontation with sexuality, or, specifically, *homo*sexuality. "The escape from parental authority was bound to bring to the fore not simply the rediscovery of the physical beauty of the landscape but logically also the physical beauty of man's body, thus breaking the taboo which had surrounded the entire problem of sexuality. . . . The call to the return to nature was bound to produce the ultimate confrontation between the individual and his own sexuality," says Koch.[8]

Youth movement members who were of a homosexual persuasion lived their personality-formative years in an ambiance that was ruggedly masculine and rejective of societal influences that would have stamped and branded them as counterfeit and effeminate males. The mass of German straights in large measure accepted this gay-verity image because there simply was no other existing nationwide image of gays. Nevertheless, German straights denounced gays for the usual "lifestyle" reasons when they found the lisping, wilting-pansy image did not apply.

Reports are divided over the extent of homosexuality in the *Wandervögel.* At one extreme are those who say, with Koch, "The contention . . . that the German youth movement was essentially a homoerotic movement, or more crudely a club for homosexuals, is blatant nonsense, for which there is no evidence whatsoever."[9] At the other extreme are those who maintain that the youth movement began and flourished as a product of homoerotic attraction. The latter seems to nudge nearer the truth. Regardless of what a young person's sexual orientation is, it is widely understood that during adolescence homoerotica is a powerful and nigh universal presence. Granted, this homoerotica is quite distinct from homosexualness, which should be understood to mean a rather fixed erotic desire for members of one's own sex. However, both homoerotica and homosexuality are germane because both were decidedly present in the German youth movement.

Hans Blüher, an anti-Semitic German homosexual, stirred up a sensation in 1912 with the publication of his tremendous bestseller, *The German Wandervögel Movement as an Erotic Phenomenon.* Through an ingeniously syncretic approach to the writings of Freud, Plato, Nietzsche, and Friedländer, Blüher devised a compelling analysis of the youth movement as a candid acknowledgment of homoerotic attraction among its members. Incidentally, Blüher is an example of the paradox of a German homosexual being anti-Semitic, and Blüher was a brilliant man. Blüher's case further helps explain why many Nazi gays were attracted to Hitler and his shrill anti-Semitism, for many gentile homosexuals were rabidly anti-Semitic. Bear in mind, though, that anti-Semitic Nazi gays saw nothing more amiss with this prejudice than otherwise decent homophobes see anything amiss in their attitude toward homosexuals. It merely illustrates the quirks of prejudice, and the irony of prejudice's victims so often being prejudice's spokesmen.

Gays in the youth movement who espoused anti-Semitism, chauvinism, and the *Führerprinzip* were not-so-incipient Fascists. They helped create a fertile ground for Hitler's Movement and, later, became one of its main sources of adherents. Hence, the many racist gays in the youth movement who joined Hitler saw nothing weirdly dichotomous, perhaps even schizoid, in becoming Nazis. The progression from youth movement *Weltanschauung* to Nazi *Weltanschauung* was seen as a "logical" step by homosexuals in the *Wandervögel.*

A substantial number of those *Wandervögel* leaders were known homosexuals, and many others were allegedly gay (or bisexual). One, Wilhelm Jansen, was forced to resign his *Wandervögel* leader's post because of his wildly gay ways. He struck out on his own and formed a counter-organization. It was constituted in 1910 as the *Jungwandervögel* (Young, or, in this case, New *Wandervögel*), which attracted about 1,500 members, all of them knowing, or soon finding out, that Jansen was a homosexual. Jansen rightly complained, according to James D. Steakley's *The Homosexual Emancipation Movement in Germany,* "that the original spirit and program of the movement was being eroded by a leadership increasingly in the hands of puritanical adults. . . . But as far as homosexuality was concerned, the *Jungwandervögel* never really put its cards on the table. Instead, it issued ambiguous pronouncements like this one, from the first issue of its official journal:

"'Now no one can deny that the need for friendship is at its strongest between the ages of twelve and twenty. Generally, the boy from a middle-class background cannot find at home the kind of relaxed, intimate involvement which he rightly demands. And that teachers at public schools become friends, true friends with their pupils—this appears only in school journals or eulogies for deceased pedagogues. But precisely this: friendly relations with an older person, who doesn't simply patronize a boy because of his inexperience . . . ; this is what made the Wandervögel great. Our binding force is not the will to comradeship but rather the will to friendship.' "[10]

Steakley explains that the "emphasis on friendship in this [the foregoing] statement gives it an unmistakable homosexual ring, particularly when one considers the nuances of the word in German (homosexual 'lovers' are called 'friends')."[11] Blüher claimed that outright homosexuality—*not* comradeship or simple friendship—was the binding force of the *Jungwandervögel* and that its original leaders had *all* been homosexual. When this disclosure was published, corrosive controversy erupted in the straight community the same as it would if a reliable authority were to announce today that the Boy Scouts of America is a playground for nancies. Charges and countercharges rent not only the *Jungwandervögel* but the entire youth movement. It is nothing but "a front for a club of pederasts," cried the moral guardians.

A sourness descended upon the youth movement. What had begun as a romantic excursion into communion with nature and the nature of one's whole self developed ugly, sexless currents of poisonous racism and belligerent nationalism. While the *Jungwandervögel* lasted (effectively up until the outbreak of World War I), it promoted a frank and healthy eroticism combined with socialism and pacifism. Most of the rest of the youth movement, however, became irreconcilably torn asunder by internal and external conflict over the issue of the sexual, including, of course, homosexual, rights of youth. Strict chastity was demanded by straights in the movement who trumpeted anti-Semitic, nationalistic, and authoritarian policies. Hans Peter Bleuel comments in his *Sex and Society in Nazi Germany*: "It was the ethic of the underling, the outlook of the authoritarian personality: anything alien to me and forbidden by my superiors is abnormal. . . . Themselves typical of this mentality, the National Socialist rulers used it as a foundation for their edifice of tyranny by wholesome popular sentiment."[12]

The truth of just how gay was the German youth movement probably falls somewhere between the extremes of the ostensibly sexless Boy Scouts' image on the one hand and homosexual clubbiness on the other. It was a shade of gray—not black or white. The youth movement was not a homosexual cabal, but there probably was a greater number of gay sex encounters and love affairs in the youth movement than there might have been otherwise, especially in its early days before authoritarian straight youths and adults clamped down on *Wandervögel* eros. Doubtless, the youth movement milieu was conducive to homoerotic contact, and perhaps nurtured an appreciation for bisexual expression, but it seems unlikely that it created any significant increase in the average number of card-carrying homosexuals in light of Kinsey's findings.

While the number of gays and the extent of homosexual behavior in the youth movement are moot questions, there is no question about its nascent Fascism and chauvinism. The movement deteriorated into jingoistic and moralistic parodies of what it once was and stood for—a robust, healthy, happy communion with and between "I and Thou" and Nature.

"Such was the state of mental unpreparedness and confusion of the organized German Youth Movement, helplessly dispersed in hundreds of fractions and groups, rotten in some sections with the poison of anti-Semitism and chauvinism, which created the most favorable conditions for the cold-bloodedness and singlemindedness of the Nazis, who applied their technique of infiltration and substituted by cunning and force their own Fascist creed. *The result was the disintegration of the German Youth Movement into the Hitler Youth* [original italics]," says J. G. Siebert in *The Re-Making of German Youth.*[13]

Had the movement stuck to its original philosophy, minus the Volk, Reich, and Führer business, there might have grown up enough sane and loving Germans to jeer Hitler, even in the country's social and economic distress, and thereby destroy him. The words "What might have been" are sad indeed. The dream that straight and gay German youth pursued when they so blithely marched off to war in 1914 would be the same deceiving and devouring dream they would pursue when many of them began marching behind Hitler in 1919. Not until 1934 would Nazi gays become aware of their misreading of reality.

Anti-Nazi homosexuals who led the pre-1933 German gay movement (in 1933 it ceased to exist), or sympathized with it, were anxiously aware of the Nazi threat. Straight Nazi SA men harassed and beat gay movement leaders and supporters and demolished a number of the movement's offices.

After June 30, 1934, both Nazi and anti-Nazi gays were consumed by Hitler's dragon, the teeth of which were becoming ever longer, sharper, and bloodier.

4

Juggernaut

When Germany's youth limped back from the death-stinking trenches of World War I they found nothing to come home to. There were no cheers and bands and parades and flags to wave them home. They were met with hostility or sullen indifference. They were called cowards and blamed for having lost the war.

The bad got worse: On the day the Armistice was signed in the forest of Compiègne, November 11, 1918, the German mark stood at 7.45 to the dollar. Five years later, in November of 1923, the German mark stood at 4,210,500,000,000 to the dollar. A German lawyer took out an insurance policy for 1,000,000 marks in 1903. When it matured in 1923, he took the proceeds and bought a single loaf of bread. Beggars threw away 100,000-mark notes. The price of a pair of shoelaces would a few weeks earlier have bought the entire store and stock. Factories, apartment houses, office buildings could be had for about $20 apiece (U.S. currency).

Inflation's disruptive effect struck a nation already demoralized and disoriented, for it followed in the wake of a nine-year period that included the war, a revolution, the Kapp Putsch, and the occupation of the Ruhr. It coincided with the feverish mood of a postwar society that seemed to have thrown off the restraints of the past. In Berlin and other cities there was seen an orgy of dancing, drinking, and sexual debauch. The gaiety concealed thinly (or not at all) a gnawing anxiety about the future amidst a nightmarish background of poverty, unemployment, and despair.

Inflation permitted foreigners to live in luxury hotels for almost nothing under the eyes of starving Germans. The streets were filled with begging, often mutilated ex-servicemen. Children were sent to beg or steal or prostitute themselves to get money for food. The birth rate plunged, and death, suicide, illness, and abortion rates skyrocketed. The middle classes were dealt a tremendous moral and material blow, and it shattered their confidence, never very great, in the Republic. From the ranks of the disinherited bourgeoisie much future support for Hitler was to come. Those living on fixed incomes and pensions (if any), including over a million war widows, were cast adrift.

E. Y. Hartshorne says in *German Youth and the Nazi Dream of Victory*: "The impression made on youth at this time was all the blacker because of material, as well as psychic, disturbances. . . . There were . . . strikes, military revolts and even intermittent civil war; machine-gun fire could be heard in city streets; there were dead and wounded; houses were destroyed. Then came the inflation, which wiped out the last vestiges of middle class security. The result was enhanced 'flight from reality' in the direction of the 'dream of national glory.' As far as youth were concerned this flight from reality expressed itself all through the so-called Youth Movement. . . ." Hartshorne reports one of its members as saying: " 'We little suspected then what power we had in our hands. We played with the fire that had set a world in flames, and it made our hearts hot. Mysticism and everything mystical had dominion over us. It was in our ranks that the word *Fuehrer* originated, with its meaning of blind *obedience* and devotion. The word *Bund* arose with us too, with its mysterious undertone of conspiracy. And I shall never forget how in those early days we pronounced the word *Gemeinschaft* [unity, oneness] with a trembling throaty note of excitement, as though it hid a deep secret.' "[1]

They got their Führer in a man out of nowhere, a high school drop-out, Adolf Hitler, who was not even a German; he was an Austrian, and did not obtain German citizenship until February 25,

1932, the year in which the Nazis became the largest political party in Germany. Their Führer gave straight and gay youth the *Gemeinschaft* it so yearned for. This Führer, the Iron Cross-decorated World War I hero, also provided his fellow war veterans—who were mostly in their twenties—outlets for their frustration and rage. He restored their dignity as men, convincing them they had not been defeated but betrayed. It was the lost generation of German youth, straight and gay and seething with discontent, and for awhile still bound by the homoerotic brotherhood of the trenches, who paved Hitler's royal road to power in the rubbish-and-ruin-strewn aftermath of the war.

There is ample confirmation of the Nazi Movement's youthfulness. German historian Friedrich Meinecke says that Hitler came to power through a typical but dazzled and blinded youth movement. A former high-ranking Nazi, Albert Krebs, states, "The years of my membership in the Nazi party brought me into contact with most of its leaders at the upper and intermediate levels. . . . What one noticed primarily was that they were very young, with all the advantages and disadvantages of youth."[2] According to British historian A. J. Ryder, "The Nazis could present themselves as the party of youth, with the confidence and dynamism of men unhindered by the fears and inhibitions of middle age. And Germany was presented as the youngest, and therefore the most vigorous, of the great powers. Nearly all the Nazi leaders were young men."[3] The American historian, Robert G. L. Waite, writes, "Members of Hitler's own generation, born in the 1890s, gave him broad support whether they were shopkeepers or journalists, soldiers or peasants, priests or professors. But those who turned to him with particular fervor were the sons and daughters of this generation—those, born during and shortly after the Great War, who would become the radical youth of 1930-1933. These juveniles and adolescents were of the utmost importance to Hitler, and he responded to their needs so effectively that one historian of the Weimar youth movement concluded, 'National Socialism came to power as the party of youth.' "[4]

Even after 1933 the Party continued to be characterized by youth. For instance, most of the SS, especially in the ranks, consisted of members between ages 18 and 20. Heinrich Himmler had been only

28 when Hitler appointed him SS Chief; Himmler, incidentally, was a notorious heterosexual; he fathered several illegitimate children. Also, most of the SS were single—93.5 percent single in 1938. These figures are for the Death's Head units (among whom were the concentration camp personnel), but generally apply as well to other SS units and the SA.

More than 42 percent of all Germans in the 18-30 age group who were members of political parties had joined the Nazi Party by 1932—the year *before* Hitler assumed power. The Social Democratic Party had less than 20 percent of the youth. In Hamburg, 66 percent of the Party members were younger than 30; in Halle the percentage was 86 percent. In the Reichstag, 60 percent of the National Socialists were under 40; among the Social Democrats only 10 percent were of that age group.

Nazism was the party of youth because in essence Nazism was a youth movement. At one Berlin rally in 1932 more than 100,000 youths gathered to hear Hitler speak, and marched past him for seven-and-a-half hours. One particularly cynical older Nazi averred that all those clean-cut, shiny-eyed automatons came out of "Adolf's toy box." In the young generation the Nazis found the population group that was the most malleable to its own purpose and one that returned the highest yield of self-sacrificing allegiance for the blandishment invested. "The Nazis . . . had been the party of Youth *versus* Age less by championing youthful causes than by uninhibited assault upon the staid Republic; when in power they instantly called off the age-war and managed to make their subsequent manipulation of the young serve two ends that were not readily reconcilable: liberating the full potential of juvenile aggressiveness, while at the same time impressing the adult public with the degree of discipline to which youth could be subjected," as Grunberger puts it.[5] It was largely a case of the young manipulating the young.

Though many youths were opportunistic, they were not, at least before 1933, nearly the band-wagoneers so many of the older Nazis were both before and after 1933. Many of the older Nazis joined the Movement because they expected to profit from it by personal gain and status inaccessible to them otherwise. Nearly all the old Party officials were men and women who believed they had nothing to lose and everything to gain by signing up with the Nazis. Had there been some other promising horse in the race besides Hitler, many of them would have put their money on that other horse.

Youth, however, was generally more impelled by idealism—and by impatience, deprivation, bitterness, blathering stupidity, and an unconscionable disregard for the rights of others. Krebs says in his memoirs, as edited by Allen: "Seen as a whole, the party was . . . an organization of 'new men' who were breaking into the domain of politics with youthful obstreperousness, full of faith in their own mission and determined to use their eagerness at risk-taking to make the impossible possible. From the spiritual heritage of the past they took whatever they thought useful for their goals and purposes. That produced, especially in the beginning, a remarkable mixture of liberal, conservative, Marxist, reactionary, and revolutionary elements. . . ."[6]

If the juxtaposition of idealism and evil seems confusing, it is because idealists who do not temper their percepts with humanity can be cruelly insensate. A German housewife said, "The ranks of the NSDAP were filled with young people. Those serious people who joined did so because they were for social justice. . . ."[7] She was not altogether wrong, but she might have added that those same youths were for social justice *except* for Jews, and, if homophobic, were for social justice *except* for homosexuals.

As for others, the hope for a solution to the economic crisis gave Hitler the leadership of a nation that had not bargained for another war or for all of the despicable deeds of the Nazi era. One may even wonder to what extent Hitler envisaged the course he was to pursue. It is at least possible to suppose that he himself did not understand fully the savagery of which he was capable. There is no question that countless young gays and straights did *not* have their heart in what they were doing. They marched to Hitler's tune not out of dedication but in fear. "There were many who camouflaged themselves like endangered animals, out of a pure instinct for survival. They howled with the wolves to keep from being torn to pieces," said the disenchanted Nazi Gauleiter Albert Krebs.[8]

The anomaly of gays joining with and supporting gay-haters sprung not only from fear or stupidity but also arose from the fact that no one likes to be an outsider, and that in truth their similarities with other members of the *Volk* probably greatly outnumbered their dissimilarities. At rock bottom all of us are more alike than we are different, which was particularly true of the Germans, among whom the authoritarian-personality type was rife. This is one reason why an authoritarian Hitler was so in tune with the authoritarian German masses—gay and straight—and why he and they so closely identified with each other.

Hitler was the archetype of the authoritarian personality. Such a person admires the strong, is contemptuous of the weak, insists on blind obedience to his authority, demands conformity, glorifies himself, and rejects those who are different or who are outsiders as being either a threat or scum or both. He praises unrelenting toughness and determination and adopts that posture as an ego ideal, and rigidly separates masculinity from femininity. Such a person is frequently inconsistent and illogical, and often enraged because the inelasticity of his mental-emotional set usually does not brook negotiation or accommodation; his inflexibility does not tolerate much disparity in people, thought, or behavior. Hence, he will say and do things contrary to logic and consistency in an attempt to force or otherwise impose his brand of thinking and conformity upon the world around him. Because weakness would undermine his brittle personality superstructure, he despises and fears it in himself and others. To reduce or exorcize anxieties resulting from feelings of weakness, the authoritarian personality will project onto others the mantle of weakness and whatever else he perceives as despicable or fearful within himself. Also, by doing this, the condemnation of others feeds an ever-present hunger for a compensatory need to feel superior; sympathy for the weak cannot develop, for there is an ingrained fear of weakness that serves as a target for aggression and at the same time fuels a fierce need to dominate others.

Nazi gays up to 1934 seemingly occupied a congenial situation because Hitler led them into fooling themselves that his *Volksgemeinschaft* laid down the welcome mat for homosexuals. Was not the most outstanding, most *notorious,* of all homosexuals the celebrated Nazi leader Ernst Röhm, the virile and manly Chief of the SA, the *du* buddy of Adolf Hitler from the beginning of his political career? Hitler's rise had in fact depended upon Röhm, and everyone knew it. Röhm's gay fun and games were certainly no secret; his amorous forays to gay bars and gay Turkish baths were riotous. Whatever anti-homosexual sentiments may have been expressed by straight Nazis were more than offset by the reality of highly visible, spectacular, gay-loving Röhm. If there were occasional ominous rumblings and grumblings about "all those queers" in the SA and Movement, and some anti-gay flare-ups, homosexual Nazis felt more or less secure in the lap of the Party. After all, the National Socialist Party member who wielded the greatest power aside from Hitler was Röhm.

Röhm's lifestyle was so well known that the inevitable jokes about him and the SA circulated throughout Germany. A widespread joke about the gay bent of the SA, which made homophobic Nazis and SA men flinch, had to do with the routine progression, or "graduation," of boys and young men from the Hitler Youth to the ranks of the SA: "Out of the Hitler Youth an SA Man Will Emerge!" was a popular motto until both gays and straights began to burst into laughter upon hearing it.

Master psychologist Hitler got it both ways: He enlisted gay-hating straights and gay-loving gays under one flag. Hitler's Juggernaut of Youth is a deadly accurate characterization in its applicability to young Nazi gays in particular and German youth in general. "Juggernaut" refers to an idol drawn on an enormous cart under whose wheels devotees are said to have thrown themselves to be crushed; anything to which a person blindly devotes himself, or is cruelly sacrificed; any large, relentless, destructive force; an institution, or nation, to which persons blindly sacrifice themselves or others.

Adolf Hitler at about age 30 when he embarked on what he declared was his "historic mission of destiny." He was a handsome man at the time. In fact, he was frequently called *Der Schöne Adolf* (the handsome Adolf), a descriptive and affectionate term used by girls and women. Many regarded the *Führer* as an attractive sex symbol. His masculine good looks were also to some extent helpful in gaining big-money support from Ernest Röhm's circle of wealthy gay friends. *(National Archives Photo)*

"German youth, I salute you!" roared the *Führer* to his *Hitler Jugend* (Hitler Youth). Homosexuals did not fit Hitler's notion of what Teutonic Supermen of the Master Race ought to be: "Slim and strong," demanded Hitler, "and as fast as a grayhound, as tough as leather, and as hard as Krupp steel." *(National Archives Photo)*

Reich Legal Director Hans Frank fondly pats a Hitler Youth boy who has just presented him with flowers. If that boy had been discovered to be a homosexual, then or later, he could expect no mercy. Frank once said, "Particular attention should be addressed to homosexuality, which is clearly expressive of a disposition opposed to the normal national community. Homosexual activity means the negation of the community as it must be constituted if the race is not to perish. That is why homosexual behavior, in particular, merits no mercy."

The International Military Tribunal on war crimes never specifically investigated the Nazi extermination of homosexuals. Consequently gays were excluded from reparations after the war. Gays were seen by all authorities concerned as felonious violators who, yet again, merited no mercy. *(National Archives Photo)*

Hitler Youth boys read a Nazi publication prepared especially for them. Boys who became sexually chummy were often treated the same as any older homosexual: imprisonment, abuse, and extermination. *(National Archives Photo)*

The *Führer* reviews the Hitler Youth at a Party rally. "I want hard and cruel youths from whom the world will shrink back in terror," he said. He ordered the youth organization "cleansed" of homosexuals so that every German mother could rest assured that her son would not be homosexually corrupted in its ranks. The persecution of homosexuals notwithstanding, the Hitler Youth was covertly referred to throughout Germany as the "Homo Youth." *(National Archives Photo)*

A candid shapshot of Ernst Röhm, in the foreground. Peering over Röhm's shoulder is SA Berlin Leader Karl Ernst. A very dashing and handsome figure, the bisexual Karl Ernst was popular with both females and males. *(Library of Congress Photo)*

SA Chief of Staff Ernst Röhm. His face was scarred by bullet wounds in World War I, when he served in the trenches as an Army captain. *(Library of Congress Photo)*

Ernst Röhm, center, and Edmund Heines, right, with an unidentified officer. Heines was always at Röhm's side—in more ways than one. *(National Archives Photo)*

The crack of pistol shots shattered the peaceful and sleepy early morning stillness on Saturday, June 30, 1934, at the Hotel Hanselbauer (lower right at the lake's edge) in the resort health spa at Bad Wiesee, Germany, where an hysterical *Führer* arrested SA Chief Ernst Röhm, and, it seems, found SA General Edmund Heines in bed with his handsome male chauffeur, apparently caught in the act of having sex. (Contrary to many reports, Hitler and his entourage did not burst into the hotel with guns blazing but crept in, "almost on tiptoe," said one eyewitness.) They were immediately shot, with Heines at first shouting loud and angry objections that quickly changed to subdued pleading for his life. The Blood Purge had begun about two hours earlier at the Ministry of the Interior in Munich with the summary shooting of two SA officers at point blank range while they attempted to welcome Hitler to the Ministry. Hitler kicked one of the corpses and remarked, "These men were not the most guilty!" Thus began the Blood Purge that was to end in the genocide of homosexuals. *(National Archives Photo)*

Herman Göring, left, and Heinrich Himmler taking a rare stroll. They detested and feared each other, but it was these two who hatched the Blood Purge that culminated in the extermination of homosexuals throughout Nazi-controlled Europe. *(National Archives Photo)*

5

Blood Purge

"That night [January 30, 1933, when Hitler was appointed Chancellor by President Paul von Hindenburg], for hours on end, thousands and thousands of Stormtroopers [SA] marched through Berlin to celebrate the Nazi victory," writes Robert Goldston in *The Life and Death of Nazi Germany*. "Their bands played the old German martial airs, their drums boomed, the tramp of their jackboots shook the pavement, while the thousands of flaming torches they carried gave them the appearance of some army marching out of the dark ages of human history. On the Wilhelmstrasse, at the windows of the Chancellery building, Adolf Hitler responded with his outstretched arm salute as the guttural roar of '*Sieg Heil!*' (Hail Victory!) resounded through the night. And the German crowds, in their thousands, cheered the marching Stormtroopers. If there were any among them who felt the forebodings which such a scene must have aroused in the breast of any sane or civilized human being, they were careful to keep their silence. On that night of January 30, 1933, Germany plunged happily, deliriously, joyfully into an abyss from which she has not yet fully emerged"[1]: From which thousands of German gays and those in Nazi-occupied territories never emerged.

The SA had made the greatest single contribution to preparing the groundwork for Hitler's rise to power, and, until the 1934 Blood Purge, of keeping him in power. On that ecstatic night of January 30, 1933, Hitler's eyes glittered with sincere gratitude in his salute to the SA boys in the *Bund.* Hitler himself declared many times before 1933 that if his Party won the struggle for power it would be thanks to the SA. It was not all that simple, but there can be no gainsaying that Hitler became a political energumen through the massive force of the SA.

The divergence in interpreting gay influence in the history of the Party lies in the fact that until June-July 1934 the SA was dominated by homosexuals at the top, so it is very easy to conclude that Nazism was the poisonous product of homosexuals. No matter how educated, erudite, and eminently qualified historians and others may be who expound on Hitler and the Third Reich, many astonishingly fail to grasp the full import of the most elementary fact: Hitler was first, last, and always a politician desperately clawing for total power. Everyone knows this. Yet when it comes to his toleration of gays before, and to a minuscule extent after, the Blood Purge, most seem to ignore that quintessential fact about Hitler. Homosexuals were Hitler's personal and political unresolved problem, one he did not squarely face until June 30, 1934, *after* he had gained the power he sought, partly through the efforts and sacrifices of many homosexuals.

Gays as such were never asked to join the SA and Party or work for it in any way whatever. But they did join and they did work for the Cause, except, of course, for those gays who opposed Nazism or who were indifferent to it. Among Nazi gays were those who actually felt the National Socialist Revolution would fully bring about gay emancipation; Hitler was not about to cut their throats until he could do it without cutting his own.

Most people never question the "partnership" Hitler formed with heterosexuals, but many make much ado about the "partnership" he formed with homosexuals. Nazi straights per se are never seen as immoral because they were straight, but Nazi gays per se are usually always considered immoral because they were gay. The following passage exemplifies the turned-inside-out double-standard thinking that slides by most heterosexual commentators but comes to a screeching halt with regard to homosexuals. As with all such thinking, it is automatically assumed that homosexuality equals immorality. Hitler is always "blamed" for the presence and pre-1934 domination of gays, but never "blamed" for the presence and domination of heterosexuals:

"Q. *Is it true that Hitler is a homosexual?*

"A. No, it is not true. He came seriously under suspicion because of his intimacy with Roehm, and because for so many years he tolerated the blatant homosexuality of Roehm and his cohorts. This was a scandal so colossal that it surely has no counterpart in history. Roehm as the head of 2,500,000 Storm Troops had surrounded himself with a staff of perverts. His chiefs, men of the rank of Gruppenfuehrer or Obergruppenfuehrer, commanding units of several hundred thousand Storm Troopers, were almost without exception homosexuals. Indeed, unless a Storm Troop officer were homosexual, he had no chance of advancement.

"All this was known to every intelligent observer in Germany and of course was known in every detail to Hitler. His moral indignation when he made his Blood Purge and cleaned out this 'nest of immorality' was one of his more brazen pieces of hypocrisy. He purged Roehm not on account of his distasteful habits but because Roehm was plotting to seize power, make himself head of the Army, and form what would have been, incidentally, a homosexual government.

"Nobody knows whether he intended to do away with Hitler or merely force Hitler to go along with him. At any rate Hitler would have no part of it, and Roehm was killed, though not for his abnormal love life. Thereafter Hitler passed the most stringent edicts against homosexuality and this odd feature of German life was driven underground. It remains, nevertheless, characteristic of the Germans, that they, outwardly the most brutally masculine of all European peoples, are the most homosexual nation on earth."[2]

Long before the Purge most straight Nazis were violently furious in their disapprobation of very-much-out-of-the-closet gays in the Party (up to 1933 all SA men were Party members). Homophobes in the SA were embarrassed and angered by gay Storm Troopers who were anything but sexually discreet. SA homosexuals' public embracing, kissing, dancing together, and wild night-life scenes in

Germany's beer halls, gay bars, and cabarets were a canker in the eyes of straights within and outside the SA. There were not all that many gays in the SA, but they were in command and a very visible eyesore to heterosexual Storm Troopers who felt tainted by homosexual jokes and comments about the SA that made the rounds in Germany. Being garbed in SA brown themselves, they were incensed by references to "brownie fairies."

Of course, the SA was not the only place where Nazi gays were to be found. However, except for unquestionable cases of a person's heterosexuality, homosexuality, or bisexuality, one must be skeptical or at the least circumspect about taking as fact what some writers say about certain individuals' sexual orientation and/or sexual activities.

Depending on what writer one happens to be reading at any given moment, "some Nazis were sexual perverts," "a number of Nazis were sexual perverts," "many Nazis were sexual perverts," "most Nazis were sexual perverts," "all Nazis were sexual perverts." Reportedly, Hitler Youth Leader Baldur von Schirach was bisexual; Hitler's private attorney, Reich Legal Director, Minister of Justice, butcher Governor-General of Poland, and public gay-hater Hans Frank was said to be a homosexual; Hitler's adjutant Wilhelm Brückner was said to be bisexual; Party Deputy Rudolf Hess, the Number 3 man in the hierarchy before his flight to Scotland to seek British collaboration with the Nazis against the Russians, who was often snickeringly called Fräulein Hess in Germany, was said to be bisexual; Walther Funk, Reich Minister of Economics, has frequently been called a "notorious" homosexual—or as a jealous predecessor in Funk's post, Hjalmar Schacht, contemptuously claimed, Funk was a "harmless homosexual and alcoholic"; Hermann Göring liked to dress up in drag and wear campy makeup; and so on and so forth. One astute observer said he would not venture to hazard whether the rumored gayness of certain Nazis was or was not true: "I wouldn't know. I never slept with those men."

There are any number of cases in which allegations of sexual "deviation" are either true or probably true, but there are others in which such allegations might be suspect. The most glaring example—and almost certainly preposterous—is the case of Hitler himself. Samuel Igra points out in *Germany's National Vice* (homosexuality) that there exists documentary evidence that Adolf Hitler "had been a male prostitute in Vienna at the time of his sojourn there, from 1907 to 1912, and that he practiced the same calling in Munich from 1912 to 1914."[3] (In 1907 Hitler was 18; Louis L. Snyder says Hitler left Vienna in May 1913 for Munich, which at the time was as gay, in the homosexual sense of the word, as was Berlin.) Hermann Rauschning, an erstwhile high-ranking Nazi, was reported to have read the documents, and Benito Mussolini supposedly possessed a copy of them. (This, supposedly, was one of the reasons Mussolini was in the beginning disdainful of Hitler. The Italian dictator was very much the heterosexual. Instead of having coffee-breaks, he would have sex with his female secretaries on the floor of his office.) Regardless of the assumed authenticity of the allegations, in this case there surely can be no question that the documents concerning Hitler's homosexual hustling were false—if, indeed, such documents ever really existed.

Another example is the Grynszpan case. Here, however, the charge of homosexuality was possibly true. At least, no evidence has been brought forward affirming or refuting that the Grynszpan case was due to a homosexual love affair that had a tragic ending: Seventeen-year-old Herschel Grynszpan, an exceedingly handsome youth with the sensitive looks of the late Sal Mineo, with eyes just as huge and dark and expressive, walked into the German Embassy in Paris on November 7, 1938, pulled out a pistol, and shot Ernst vom Rath, German Embassy Counsellor. Vom Rath died on November 9, 1938.

Reportedly, the shooting occurred as a consequence of a law that took effect October 31, 1938, in which the Polish government revoked the citizenship of Polish Jews who had been living abroad for more than five years and who still retained Polish citizenship. The Polish government quite simply wanted no more Jews, thousands of whom would return to Poland if expelled by Germany. At this time there were about 15,000 Polish Jews in Germany, and the Nazis did not want to get "stuck" with them. Berlin asked Poland to take its Jews back, but Poland refused. Grynszpan's family, who had been in Germany for years (Herschel's father, a Polish Jew, had been in Germany for twenty-seven years), was among those Polish

Jews declared Stateless; Herschel Grynszpan at the time was in Paris staying with an uncle. The Nazis, in response to the Polish action and refusal, ordered the arrest of all 15,000 Polish Jews in Germany for deportation to Poland on the night of October 29-30, 1938. Thousands, including Grynszpan's family, were herded into makeshift camps in a no-man's land along the border region of Zbonszyn in freezing weather.

Grynszpan's murder of Rath was claimed by the Nazis to be the spark that ignited the "spontaneous" pogrom against Jews in Germany on November 9, 1938, the so-called Crystal Night (*Kristallnacht*), in which Jewish shops, synagogues, and homes were burned or smashed and ransacked; at least 1,000 Jews were killed and 26,000 were flung into concentration camps. A great many of the dead were men, women, and children the Nazis called "Flying Jews"—those whom the Nazis laughingly threw out of windows or off roof tops. Actually, the pogrom had been planned by Hitler, Göring, Himmler, Heydrich, and Goebbels well in advance of Rath's murder. It was so propitious an incident that some believed Rath had been killed in a Nazi plot.

The French Vichy government released Grynszpan to the Germans in 1940 (actually, the Gestapo hunted him down and seized him). The Nazis geared up for a spectacular show trial, which was scheduled for May 1942. At the last moment the trial was canceled on Hitler's orders: Grynszpan had threatened to reveal a homosexual relationship with Rath. According to *Crystal Night,* by Rita Thalmann and Emmanuel Feinermann, Goebbels wrote in his journal: "Grynszpan has insolently invented a homosexual liaison with Embassy Counsellor vom Rath [whom Goebbels called "a young handsome Aryan"]. It is nothing other than a shameless fabrication. But it is a lucky inspiration for him, since if it were brought out in a trial it would become a dominant theme in adverse propaganda."

No one knows what was going through Grynszpan's head when he shot Rath. The plight of Grynszpan's family when cruelly ejected from Germany at gun-point—stripped of nearly everything except a few German marks for "traveling money"—might have been uppermost, particularly if in fact he was having an affair with a German diplomat, an affair that might have been on the rocks before the Polish-German issue arose. In any event, it seems likely the Gestapo investigated and found Grynszpan's assertion that he was having an affair with Rath was probably true. Had this emerged in a trial it would have sullied Rath, the Nazis, and soiled the Crystal Night pogrom with "faggotism." After all, one does not stage a "spontaneous" righteously wrathful pogrom just over a couple of homosexuals who had a lovers' quarrel.

Aside from such cases that are more-or-less substantiated, there are insurmountable problems in pinning down facts in that sexually murky bygone era. Most of the principals or those who knew the facts have been murdered, took their own lives, or perished in other ways. And that says nothing of the destroyed records and the persons who could talk but never will, particularly not about homosexuality, and certainly not if it would or might implicate themselves or their friends. Even when "documentary" evidence is cited, facts are still elusive, an example of which involves the alleged bisexuality of Reinhard Heydrich, SD* (Security Service) Chief in the SS.

Admiral Wilhelm Canaris, head of Abwehr, the Foreign Intelligence and Counterintelligence Department of the High Command of the Armed Forces, who was a leader in the July 20, 1944, conspiracy against Hitler, was said to have a dossier on Heydrich's homosexual activities after the latter had been cashiered from the Navy. In his early twenties Heydrich served as an officer in the German Navy, from which he was dismissed in 1931 after a courtmartial for having an affair with a young girl who had parents in high places. Incidentally, Canaris's Abwehr also reportedly discovered that Heydrich's father, a singer, was a *Mischling*, a part-Jew. This was in the dossier, too. In light of Canaris's known penchant for integrity of sorts, the material in the dossier was probably true. Officially or by stealthy design, the file found its way to Himmler and then to Hitler.

Heydrich, meanwhile, was busily creating dossiers himself. He produced counterfeit evidence against the German Army's Commander-in-Chief, Werner von Fritsch, who stood in the way of the Nazification of the Armed Forces, bringing the victim down with charges of sexual perversion. Fritsch did not actually oppose the Nazis and Hitler. The Commander-in-Chief strung along with

*The origin of this abbreviation is in the German original, *Sicherheitsdienst.*

them but had an independent bent of mind and, worse, was an old-fashioned Army officer who felt that the dignity of the military should not be compromised by politics, and that the Armed Forces should be held aloof with its power on virtually an autonomously equal footing with the State. In other words, he wanted soldiering left to the soldiers and politics left to the politicians. That is definitely not what Hitler wanted. Fritsch had to be gotten out of the way so that the Wehrmacht* could be more easily subjugated to the Party's and Hitler's will. Though Fritsch was eventually cleared of the phony charge, he was nevertheless forced to resign on February 4, 1938. After Fritsch's good name was restored by a military court of honor, Hitler wrote to him, "I can imagine how much those reproaches must have weighed on you; be assured that such an idea made me suffer ceaselessly, too." That was not altogether an outright lie, for Hitler was initially averse to opening up such a crucial scandal. (The letter was put up for sale in 1979 in Hamburg, Germany, and fetched $3,250.)

In 1937-1938 Hitler still did not feel sufficiently secure of his power over the Armed Forces to take preemptive action against it and its top officers (later, he would simply have officers shot out of hand). So, while the case against Fritsch was brewing, Hitler resorted to heterosexual scandal to get rid of Field Marshal Werner von Blomberg, Minister of War and Commander-in-Chief of the Wehrmacht. He, too, was forced to resign, on February 4, 1938. He was charged with disgracing the Officer Corps by marrying a young, pretty typist-secretary in the War Ministry, Erna Gruhn, who, it seems, was for hire as a shady lady of the night.

The plot and details behind the Fritsch-and-Blomberg "Crisis" are too thick and tangled to go into here. Suffice to say, the outcome allowed Hitler to solidify his control over the Armed Forces and embark upon his program of global aggression. Hitler abolished the Ministry of War in February 1938, and, after getting Fritsch, Blomberg, and sixteen other generals out of the way, he appointed himself Commander-in-Chief of the Armed Forces, which further

---

*Wehrmacht was the official name of the combined Army, Navy, and Air Force in the Third Reich. Under the *Wehrgesetz* (defense law) decreed by Hitler on May 21, 1935, the term Reichswehr, used to describe the 100,000-man Army of the Weimar Republic, was replaced by Wehrmacht.

consolidated the power he already held as its Supreme Commander in his position of President and Chancellor.

To return to the file material Canaris reportedly had on Heydrich's homosexual activities: It may have been legitimate or it may have been fabricated, just as Heydrich fabricated the case against Fritsch, although informed conjecture suggests that the Heydrich dossier was accurate. Canaris was mortally afraid of Heydrich, for very good reasons, and obviously wanted a weapon he could use against him. It appears that everyone except Hitler was frightened of Heydrich, whether or not they had clear cause to be. Himmler is said to have heaved a sigh of relief when Heydrich, Himmler's subordinate, was fatally wounded by partisans on May 27, 1942, in Liben, Czechoslovakia. Heydrich died, agonizingly, on June 4th.

While digressive, it is interesting to note that the relationship between Canaris and Heydrich was a curious one. Heydrich's SD was originally formed to function as the domestic intelligence branch of the SS. The SD and Abwehr were not supposed to be rivals, but in fact they were rivals for supremacy in the field of espionage, domestic and foreign. Oddly, Canaris and Heydrich appeared to be the best of friends. Their Berlin homes were close together, and they and their families constantly visited one another. Nevertheless, although Canaris was never nervous or intimidated in Hitler's presence, a mere nonsocial, official telephone call from Heydrich could wreck Canaris's whole day. Karl Abshagen, Canaris's early biographer, said:

"Canaris was frankly scared to death of Heydrich. Everything about the fellow was sinister and made Canaris uneasy. He was too big for comfort. His cold, penetrating eyes set deeply in his almost mongoloid features had the frozen glint of a snake. Canaris always felt in Heydrich's presence the reality of evil, that his personality had none of the usual human limitations and that he was an evil-doer of the highest order. Yet he was fascinated, virtually mesmerized by the high intelligence of his companion, whom he once called 'the cleverest of the beasts.'"[4]

Heydrich's SD, besides the Gestapo,* was the most feared and

---

*The name "Gestapo" is taken from the German *Geheime Staats Polizei*, meaning Secret State Police, which was formed by Göring.

fearful organization in the Third Reich. Homosexuals were one of the prime targets of the SD because Heydrich—who answered only to Himmler and Hitler—was the executive in charge of the *overall* program to exterminate homosexuals, Jews, and others, a job he relished and performed with zealous speed and remarkable efficiency. He set up SD Section II-S for the "Control of Homosexuality and Abortion."

Although his Party enemies alleged that Heydrich was a part-Jew and a bisexual, Hitler considered him the ideal Nazi, and Nazi inner circles regarded Heydrich as a likely successor to Hitler even though Hermann Göring was officially slated for the post of Führer. Had things turned out differently, Heydrich, possibly part-Jew and certainly Jew murderer, and possibly part-time homosexual and certainly homosexual murderer, might have become Führer of the Third Reich—and there is no question that as Führer he would have continued to kill Jews and gays.

While Canaris was said to have a brief alleging Heydrich's homosexuality, the successor to Heydrich's post of SD Chief, Ernst Kaltenbrunner, believed that Canaris was a masochist, a sadist, and a homosexual of both active and passive character at the same time. But this must be viewed as a jaundiced adjudgment because Kaltenbrunner and other members of the top echelon of the SD hated and mistrusted Admiral Canaris and the Abwehr, believing them not only to be engaged in treasonable activities but also to be a center of every vice. Kaltenbrunner once said that 80 percent of the Abwehr were sexually perverted and could be bribed. That hardly seems an objective appraisal.

Winnowing the truth from such slander is difficult. For instance, the gay "witness" against Fritsch dug up by Heydrich's SD was a young and handsome professional criminal named Otto Schmidt. (Some sources give his name as Hans Schmidt.) He was the head of a group of blackmailers and had made his living for years by starting affairs with homosexuals so that he could blackmail them. Schmidt had stuffed Gestapo and SD files with accusations of homosexuality against many prominent persons, but, of course, it cannot be assumed that Schmidt always told the truth, as he did not tell the truth about Fritsch. His actions may have been motivated by a mistaken notion that if he cooperated with the authorities to the hilt—and beyond—he could save his neck. Schmidt accused Nazi Economics Minister Dr. Walther Funk of being gay (which was true), as well as a former German ambassador, one SS Police-President of Potsdam, and the famous international tennis star, Baron Gottfried von Cramm.

Hitler knew about Funk, a "notorious" homosexual, when he appointed him Reich Minister of Economics on February 5, 1938, the day after he got rid of Fritsch on a charge of homosexuality. "All this was clear proof that Hitler was quite unmoved by the presence or absence of homosexuals among his adherents," says Peter Hoffmann, author of *The History of the German Resistance*.[5] That statement is clearly nonsense, of course, but other than what already has been said about Hitler's pragmatism and the duality of his nature, there will be no further attempt here to try to explain what may be the inexplicable. Hitler's hero, Frederick the Great, a military genius and King of Prussia (1740-1786), was an effeminate homosexual. Indeed, why would Hitler call a suspected or proven part-gay and part-Jew, Heydrich, an ideal Nazi and consider him a likely candidate as Führer? These and other isolated cases present vagaries of a conundrum that can only be explored conjecturally, which has to some extent been done elsewhere.

Schmidt was executed in the summer of 1942 at Sachsenhausen concentration camp. Himmler wrote to Göring, "I request your agreement, dear Reich Marshal, that I should submit Schmidt's case to the Führer for his authorization to execute." Göring's marginal comment was, "Ought to have been shot *long* ago."[6]

So ended Schmidt, but the controversy over gays and bisexuals in the SA and Party raged on. Up to the June 30, 1934, Blood Purge, gays in the SA were openly homosexual because their Chief, Ernst Röhm, was openly homosexual and neither he nor they gave a damn who knew it. Wherever Röhm went he frequently had in tow six or seven youths striking in their smartness and good looks; the SA Chief presented them as his aides-de-camp. They were, but they were also his sexual playmates, as everyone knew.

By 1932 the Nazi Party had become the largest party in the Reich (but not large enough to give Hitler the majority needed to become President by popular mandate), and the SA was fully aware of its paramount role in that achievement, as Hitler publicly recognized. Without Röhm and the SA, Hitler's Party might have disintegrated long before he could become Chancellor. Hence, SA gays felt they had a right to live and love in their own fashion. They felt *they* were now in charge of the nation to the exclusion of homophobes. But, of course, they were wrong. Later, they would see just how much they misjudged the situation when Himmler dramatized the effects of homosexuality on population growth until they assumed the proportions of a threat to national survival and vowed that homosexuals would be exterminated.

The SS weekly, *Das Schwarze Korps* (The Black Corps), used banner headlines to proclaim that homosexuals were enemies of the Reich. *Das Schwarze Korps* estimated that 2,000,000 men, or 10 percent of male Germans at the "height of their physical powers," were "contaminated by this frightful legacy from the liberalistic period." The vague "height of their physical powers" qualification is an important one, for it is fairly certain that 2,000,000 is an underestimation in terms of the number of gays not included in that qualification category.

Gays were also denounced by Kurt von Schleicher—ex-General, ex-Minister, and ex-Reich Chancellor. He was once overheard to exclaim loudly and angrily in a tailor's shop: "This pack of scoundrels, these criminals, these filthy boy streetwalkers! [He was referring to young gay Storm Troopers and other gay Nazis.] Well, they'd better not come near me. I won't look on it much longer. We'll soon clear out the whole gang!"[7] Schleicher did not realize how prophetically he spoke. The whole gang *was* mostly cleared out, and he did not have to "look on it much longer." He was shot by the SS on Hitler's orders in the June 1934 Purge along with Röhm and the gay SA men Schleicher loathed so much. Not altogether what he wanted, to be sure, but at least he got part of his desire fulfilled.

Not so strangely, Röhm and Schleicher at times got together and had what appeared to be cordial relations. However, this was purely politics, just as many people often consort with someone they detest, putting on a glad face when at heart only intense dislike is felt. While Schleicher and Röhm did politick together, they did not plot Hitler's overthrow as Hitler claimed in his July 13, 1934, address of vindication of the Blood Purge before the Reichstag in

Berlin's Kroll Opera House. The opera house was used because, as some historians believe, the Nazis had covertly set fire to the Reichstag building in Berlin on February 27, 1933, in a maneuver to establish dictatorial powers for Hitler, which he did acquire as a consequence of the fire. (The opera house was in part probably selected because it appealed to Hitler's theatrical grandiosity.) A young Dutchman, Marinus Van der Lubbe, was accused of setting the fire; he was also accused of being a homosexual. The Nazis convicted him and employed an executioner wielding a short-handled wide-bladed axe to chop off Lubbe's head. Hitler had reintroduced decapitation because it fascinated him. (Headsmen in concentration camps were employed on special occasions; normally, a spring-activated—rather than gravity-activated—guillotine was used in the camps. Headsmen detailed to the camps were usually shirtless and wore a standard butcher's leather apron.) For the Lubbe beheading, the executioner was dressed in top hat, tails, and white gloves.

There can be little question that though Röhm and Schleicher thoroughly despised each other they did indeed conspire together. But, this was originally done because Hitler commanded Röhm to do it in order to get Schleicher's support before 1933. Schleicher backed Röhm's desire to take over the Armed Forces and form a People's Army of National Socialists; he did this not because he believed he could force Hitler out of the picture but because he wanted to manipulate a power position for himself so as, he said, to "guide the German ship of State into safety and tranquility," and because he wanted to try to clamp limits on Hitler's power by driving a wedge between him and the Armed Forces. Schleicher, who desired a military dictatorship of Germany, may have felt he could remove Röhm after neutralizing Hitler, and then reassume his former post as Minister of Defense. In fact, he offered to support Hitler in return for a Cabinet post as head of the Reichswehr.

Schleicher had a mania for dark and tangled intrigue—and thereby intrigued himself into the grave. He tried to use for his own ends Hitler's and the Party's popularity and strength, and Hitler, of course, knew it. Schleicher, a womanizer, was a treacherous and friendless intriguer who had contempt for Röhm, partly or mostly because of his homosexuality, and felt disgust toward Hitler, whom Schleicher regarded not only as a rabble-rouser but one of the rabble itself.

Schleicher's homophobia was shared by most Nazis and Germans. Indeed, Hitler toyed with the idea of obliterating the homosexual presence as soon as he became Chancellor. "The new masters made it clear from the outset that homosexuality was prohibited in their realm of wholesome popular sentiment. A decree of 23 February 1933 banned pornographic literature of every description, likewise all public activity by the League of Human Rights. This registered association, whose motto was 'For Truth and Justice,' had constituted itself the spokesman of the homosexual minority and publicly advocated the repeal of Paragraph 175."[8] (Paragraph 175 criminalized homosexual relations.) Additionally, on February 23, 1933, a Nazi decree was issued that closed "short-time" hotels and other places frequented by homosexuals. The decree applied, of course, to gay bars, but was not enforced in all cases. Further, a number of gays were ordered castrated, some of whom survived the Holocaust. (I tracked down one such case in Europe, but the man refused to talk with me because his experience was still too emotionally painful.) Before the final solution of the homosexual problem was arrived at, Himmler considered emasculating all homosexuals.

The German gay-haters at the time certainly chose an ironic stance. There were streams of homoeroticism in male-oriented Germany that were a mile deep. It would seem that anyone could have seen for himself that gay-haters and gay-lovers were not really all too much different from each other. Perhaps the explanation is due to the simple psychology of the gay-hater loathing something he fears because of its attraction, and/or because it would force an uncomfortably new *Weltanschauung* upon him that his reactionism cannot swallow, much less digest.

Whatever the case, there was, for example, a distinct group of films having a homosexually rose-colored ethos: homoerotic films such as *Hitlerjunge Quex, Cadets, D3-88* (about an Air Force squadron in which the squad leader and his chief maintenance engineer act out the roles of loving father and mother to young handsome bright-eyed pilots), *Stukas,* and *Crew Dora.* The films were popular, but would probably now be funny embarrassments because the homoerotic element might seem so heavy-handed to us.

It is amazing how German/Nazi gay-haters used to weep, laugh, or rejoice in turn over homosexually steeped drama and then call for the extermination of homosexuals. Grunberger says in *The 12-Year Reich*: "It seems superficially paradoxical that a regime inflicting savage punishments on homosexuals should sponsor such evocations of their ethos; but the Nazi movement itself was of course essentially an all-male collective, and the cult of comradeship fostered in its formations represented a pervasive, though naturally unacknowledged, form of homosexuality."[9]

Grunberger points out that homosexual-love themes were rampant in the popular war literature of the time: "The following is a representative excerpt from Beumelburg's *Gruppe Bosemüller,* which in 1936 ranked fourth on the German booksellers' lists. The scene is a German trench on the Western Front. Corporal Wammsch has informed Private Siewers—whose nerve had given way during a recent action—that he can go on leave:

> 'But I don't want to go away . . . I have to make up for something . . . give me time, why won't you give me some time? I don't want to go home, I don't want my leave . . . I don't want it . . . I want to go back to Fleury and the Souville ravine . . . that's all I want.'
>
> He is sobbing and shaking as if in a fever.
>
> Wammsch is terribly afraid. He hadn't expected this.
>
> 'I don't want to go home . . . I'll go down on my knees before the captain . . . he will listen to me . . . I don't want to go home to my mother . . . I want to go to the Souville ravine and Fleury again.'
>
> Now he is exhausted at last. He is still sobbing and his whole body heaves. But he no longer resists. He calmly lets himself be taken into Wammsch's embrace, lets himself be caressed by Wammsch's hard hands, and there is something wonderfully dissolving in this feeling.
>
> 'There . . .' says Wammsch, deeply moved, 'I'll go straight to the captain and talk to him. Of course you'll stay with us. The first one to give you an old-fashioned look is going to get my fist in his face. . . .' "[10]

That excerpt not only represented the prevailing pattern of German war literature, it also represented the ethos of the "brotherhood of the trenches" born in World War I. It was this same brotherhood that initially became the terrorist core of the SA and the Party, formed in large part from the ranks of the paramilitary *Freikorps* (Free Corps), which, incidentally, had been organized by Schleicher. The brotherhood, however, was sundered by postwar conflict between straights and gays which grew worse as the Party grew into a national force. The dissension was initiated, as it always is, by gay-haters. Gays were not and are not anti-straight, as straights are anti-gay. Were the latter not the case, there would have been no conflict between gays and straights then or now. This conflict became severe enough to threaten Party unity and dynamism. Hitler was compelled to set aside his more-or-less yet-concealed loathing for gays and step into the breach.

In a furious tirade against Prufrocks who howled about homosexuality, Hitler tried to screw a lid on the anti-gay tempest:

"I abominate prudishness and moral prying. . . . What has it to do with our struggle? These are the outworn notions of reactionary old women like Hugenberg, who can only visualize national rejuvenation in terms of virtuous customs and austerity. 'League of Virtue' and 'Christian-German Table-Companions,' 'replacing the material losses of the nation with spiritual gains'—and all the rest of that tawdry patriotic mumbo-jumbo. Our uprising has nothing to do with bourgeois virtues. We are an uprising born of our nation's strength—the strength of its loins as well, if you like. I won't be a spoilsport to any of my men. If I demand the utmost of them, I must also permit them to let off steam as *they* please, not as it suits a lot of elderly churchhens. My lads are no angels, God knows, nor are they expected to be. I've no use for goody-goodies and League of Virtue-ites. I'm not interested in their private lives any more than I'll stand for any prying into my own private life. The Party has nothing to do with conventicles or vacuous speeches about moral rejuvenation based on the spirit and history of our nationhood."[11]

Hitler was nonetheless becoming very gravely concerned about homosexuals in the Party. In 1927 a clergyman protested in person to Hitler on behalf of outraged parents that SA Leader Edmund

Heines was having sex with teenagers in the Schill Youth, an SA-linked quasi-military youth organization. Heines had formed the group from members of a defunct *Freikorps* unit that had been organized by ex-First Lieutenant Gerhard Rossbach, whom Konrad Heiden called "the prophet of homosexuality in the National Socialist Party."

A clergyman was probably the very worst choice angered parents could have sent to Hitler to convey a complaint about Heines. Hitler hated clergymen. Nevertheless, he responded to the churchman's complaint by saying: " 'I know all that, but what am I to do? Young men must be sufficiently mature to know what they are doing. The S.A. is not a kindergarten. Whenever it is at all possible, I do protest against this swinishness. . . .' But the scandal was too flagrant. Heines could not be kept any longer. It is characteristic that Hitler only decided to intervene when Heines revolted against him personally; at a meeting of the S.A. in the *Hirschbräukeller,* the leader of the Schill Youth attacked Hitler on account of his non-military S.A. policy; this was a ground for solemn exclusion [*sic*], which the *Völkischer Beobachter* [the Party organ] announced on May 31, 1927."[12]

Officially, Heines was expelled from the SA and Party ostensibly for "loose morals." The truth is that he was kicked out because he called Hitler a "dishrag" at the Hirschbräukeller meeting and tried to stir up opposition to his leadership. During that confrontation between Hitler and Heines before hundreds of SA men at the Hirschbräukeller, Hitler temporarily let his hair down about gays in a short outburst. He shouted, "The Bratwurstglöckl clique are all 175'ers—Heines, Röhm, Zentner and all the rest of them. [175 alludes to Paragraph 175 of German law that criminalized homosexual sex acts and homosexuals.] Am I to let such people reproach me with anything!?"[13] Zentner was the proprietor of the Bratwurstglöckl tavern in Munich, a gay bar immensely popular with SA gays and other homosexuals, including Röhm and Heines.

Hitler's growing perturbation over gays, as well as the mounting fury of animosity that straights bore toward homosexuals, was increasingly becoming expressed as an illusory alarm that gays were taking over the Nazi Movement and would subvert it for their nefarious sexual purposes and indulgences. This is exactly the same thing the American correspondent Knickerbocker said about Röhm's "plot" to "seize power, make himself head of the Army, and form . . . a homosexual government." If a supposedly objective Pulitzer Prize-winning journalist, Knickerbocker, saw the situation this way before the Blood Purge, then it can be easily imagined and understood how Hitler and straight Nazis were feeling about gays in the Party, particularly SA gays, who were armed (illegally, before 1933) and thirsting for a fight.

Röhm and other homosexuals in the SA certainly had no intention of homosexualizing National Socialism. But they were tough, mean, pugnacious, and brooked no prissy interference with, or judgment about, their sex lives. Many of those gays had been in the SA from the start when Hitler formed it as a "Protection and Propaganda Troop" on August 3, 1921 (the nucleus of the SA had, however, been in the making in 1920). After October 5, 1921, the Nazi strong-arm force became known as the *Sturmabteilung* (Storm [Troop] Division). As the original name of the SA denotes, it was organized to protect National Socialist meetings, oppose rival political parties in street and meeting-place battles, and distribute propaganda material.

Men aged 18 to about 45 joined the SA, but the majority of members were in their teens and twenties. As the years of the Nazi struggle for power ground on in bloody encounters through the streets and beer halls of Germany, SA membership perforce became markedly youthful. Krebs says: "Granted that in the South the proportion of older men in the Stormtroopers was always larger than in the North because of the earlier and stronger growth of Nazism there. But by late autumn 1931 the increasing bitterness and brutalization of the struggle had led here, too, to a rapidly increasing withdrawal of the older generation. That was not just because of the obvious reluctance of men with wives and children to expose themselves to the dangers of street fighting and meeting-hall battles; the cause lay more in the difference between the reasonableness of mature men as opposed to the untrammeled wildness of young lads. One could express it more strongly: the veterans felt repelled by the rowdiness that was sometimes promoted and pampered inside the Stormtrooper units. So they withdrew, or else transferred into the so-called Reserve Stormtroopers."[14]

Albert Krebs was a Nazi ex-Gauleiter. He had a falling-out with Hitler, calling him a despot to his face, and, amazingly, lived to write about it. His attitude about young riffraff in the SA was mirrored in a conversation he had with another Nazi. The latter said every true German patriot should join the Party. "If you deliver the party over to the 'young bums' and the thugs," he explained, "then you shouldn't be surprised to see that it has fallen into bad hands."[15]

Young gays were attracted to the SA, the Party's first uniformed formation, because, as previously mentioned, they had nowhere else to go, or, rather, *felt* they had no other viable option. Along with so many others like them—the jobless, the uprooted, those to whom Weimar had become synonymous with despair—they responded and poured into the SA, which not only at first accepted them but warmly welcomed them and anyone else it could get, except Jews. The typical attitude at the time was reflected in an exchange overheard between a straight SA leader and a complaining colleague: "But they're *homosexuals!*" "So what!" replied the SA leader.

The prevailing impetus behind the rush to join the SA is crystalized in the "Song of the SA Man," which sums up the picture of masses of gays and straights striding hand-in-hand, so to speak, into the fraternity of the SA, to don its brown uniform and swastika armband, to fight, to murder, to comfortingly lick each other's wounds after every street and beer-hall battle for Hitler:

> My belly rumbled with hunger,
> I fainted and went to bed,
> Then I heard in my ears a shouting—
> 'Germany, awake!', it said.
>
> And I saw so many marching
> To the Third Reich, they cried;
> I had nothing to lose and nowhere to go,
> So I joined them and marched beside.[16]

The Party needed recruits, especially young men who were not afraid to use their fists, or a club, dagger, or pistol. So the Movement took in gays without question, just as the Party and the SA in the beginning took in former deadly enemies—Communist converts—without question. The latter had also been fighting for the establishment of a dictatorship; that is why Fascism became so appealing to erstwhile Communists. A joke that made the rounds of the SA at the time had one SA man saying to another: "In our Storm Troop unit there are three Nazis, but we shall soon get rid of them." (In the 1920s, Germany—not France or Italy—had the strongest Communist Party outside Russia.)

T. L. Jarman comments in *The Rise and Fall of Nazi Germany*: "Indeed, the violent elements in the Communist Party were attracted by the Nazis. And Röhm, it seems, welcomed them into the S.A. 'It's easier to control Communist elements inside the S.A. than by closing the ranks against them,' he said. 'They can't undermine the S.A.—some of my best men are former Communists. Let them call them 'Beefsteaks' [i.e., red inside, brown outside, as Berlin put it]. I like them radical.' "[17]

The SA and Party absorbed every willing hand, except Jews, although there were closet Jews and part-Jews in the Nazi ranks. (There were also incognito Jews in Canaris's Abwehr, friends of the Admiral, and introduced in that organization by Canaris himself under false papers.) For gays and others, the SA became a psychological home, and for those whose bellies rumbled with hunger the daily meal provided by the SA was a godsend. This was particularly true of young Storm Troopers who had no family or whose families had expelled them from home for political reasons; such cases were frequent. (There was a large silent minority of decent Germans who were so utterly appalled by Nazi hysteria and bestiality that they would disown their own sons and daughters for the sake of political and personal morality.) Aside from meals, SA men could get their uniforms and underwear that had been torn in street and beer-house brawls repaired by members of the Nazi Women's Auxiliary. Female supporters were "zealous agitators" for the Nazi cause, and within the SA found a good place to meet lovers and future husbands. Likewise, the SA also provided an excellent hunting ground and meeting place for gays seeking lovers and friends.

Once a gay or a straight entered the SA jungle, there were few practical ways of turning back. There were, of course, ways out, but the situation was something akin to becoming involved with the Mafia—options for disassociation are limited, to say the least. Krebs says, "With this party apparatus one could no longer apply the old folk wisdom that sometimes you have to howl with the wolves. Here, in order to save his own skin a man had to pull on wolves' clothing and hunt and tear with the pack. The higher the position one held the more powerfully one was subject to the rules of the machinery that one had bound oneself to."[18]

Whatever idealism one possessed initially—whether of the altruistic kind or the sledgehammer variety—became after a time irrelevant. One perforce had to run with the pack, no matter which way it ran or what it did. Nevertheless, many Nazi gays and straights were indeed "idealistic." That is what historians mean when they say that Nazism cannot be understood unless it is seen as a Movement of idealism. According to "Why," (Farrar & Rinehart, 1941) edited by Henry F. Pringle, Hitler is quoted as saying (no source is given): "Those who look upon National Socialism as a political movement misconceive its nature. It is [even] more than a religion. It is the creation of the supermen. I will free the German race from a thousand years of domestication. . . . I want to see in the eyes of youth the gleam of the beast of prey. A youth will grow up before whom the world will shrink back in terror." Idealism can thus be one man's promise and another's nightmare. In any case, once swept away in the Nazi/SA brown flood all ideals became what Hitler dictated they should be.

The SA and SS had their ideal writ large on the blades of their superbly designed and crafted daggers (which now command quite large sums of money; Himmler's SS damascus-bladed dagger, for example, a gift from Francis Xaver Schwarz, Party Treasurer and SS General, is now worth about $15,000). For the SA, the ideal was formulated in a motto acid-etched on the blades of their brown-hilted, brown-sheathed daggers: *Alles für Deutschland*—Everything for Germany. For the SS, the motto acid-etched on the blades of their black-hilted, black-sheathed daggers was *Meine Ehre heisst Treue*—My Honor is Loyalty.

In other words, according to the Nazis' own credo—which was literally and symbolically true—"Whoever pledges himself to

Hitler's banner has nothing else to call his own,"[19] including his conscience and his life.

Be that as it may, the top level of the SA and Party hierarchy came to possess a great deal they could call their own, particularly after Hitler became Chancellor. According to the study *Anatomy of the SS State,* "SA Leaders no longer went anywhere on foot. The gay [in both senses of the word] victors roared along the *Kürfurstendamm* and the *Linden* in elegant automobiles. Manufacturers or shopkeepers had presented them with these cars or put them at their disposal in order to assure themselves protection. The cars of Jews and Democrats were simply confiscated,"[20] along with many other desiderata that were in the hands of those who could not or dared not fight back. SA avarice was gangsterish, and was constrained only by SA commanders who were charged with maintaining some outward semblance of decorum, law, and order. (The SA and SS had been empowered by Hitler to act as auxiliary police; in reality, after January 30, 1933, when Hitler became Chancellor, the SA and SS were superior to the civil police and could order them about.)

The higher one went in the Party, the greater the rewards, testified Hermann Rauschning in *The Voice of Destruction,* published in 1940: "It is nothing new for a revolution to help its sons to enrich themselves, but in Germany this was done with such shameless haste that it made one dizzy to watch. One, two, or four houses, country estates, palaces, pearl necklaces, antiques, valuable tapestries and paintings, dozens of motor cars, champagne, farms, factories—where did the money come from? Had not all these people been poor as church-mice, up to their eyes in debt? They all had official posts, three, six, a dozen at a time, and always there was room for one more. There were posts of all kinds, honorary directorships, and dividends, loans and bonuses. Everyone was anxious to help: every bank and business enterprise required the protection of a party member."[21]

Ordinary German citizens did not complain openly but they did whisper. According to one source, when a parade of superluxurious cars began appearing outside public buildings in 1933 there were muted murmurings of "the new bosses are going up fast." Hitler wholeheartedly—at first—approved of all the conspicuous consumption. Nazis could become handsomely paid business "directors" and "consultants" through intimidation, although Hitler did not want Nazis deficient in the operation of business to meddle with its actual machinery. In fact, he absolutely forbade it. Otherwise, it was every top Nazi for himself. Hitler's attitude is summed up in this account reported by Rauschning:

"He [Hitler] was being reproached, he said angrily in his guttural voice, for having instituted unwarrantable prosecutions for corruption against the former rulers and their accomplices, while his own men were filling their pockets.

" 'I have answered the fools who venture to use such language to me,' he said. 'I have asked them to tell me how I could otherwise meet the justified desires of my party comrades for some recompense for their years of inhuman struggle. I have asked them whether they would prefer me to let my S.A. men loose to loot in the streets. I could still do this, I said. I had no objections. And it would be more wholesome for the people to endure a really bloody revolution for some weeks. I had refrained only out of consideration for them and their *bourgeois* love of comfort. But I could easily make up for it! They very quickly ceased making their foolish reproaches!' Hitler laughed.

" 'It is necessary to throw them into a fright now and again. I owe that to my party comrades,' he added after a pause.

" 'They have a right to demand it. After all, my party comrades have also fought to rid themselves of their personal difficulties. Preposterous not to admit it frankly. It is a duty of friendship that I should see that they all have a livelihood. My old fighting comrades have earned it. In making Germany great, we have also a right to think of ourselves. We are above clinging to *bourgeois* notions of honor and reputation. Let these 'well-bred' gentry learn that we do with a clear conscience the things they do secretly with a guilty one.'

"Growing angry, he began to shout.

" 'Are we to pull their cart out of the mud, only to be sent home with empty hands? They would like that, wouldn't they? How can I hold the power unless I have every post occupied by my men? They ought to be glad we don't shoot them, as they do in Russia!' "[22]

Lower echelons of the SA and Party, however, fared poorly for the most part because of the universalism about wealth defying gravity; wealth always rises and only a trickle seeps to the bottom. This was one of the major factors contributing to SA unrest and its desire to force into being a Socialistic nirvana through a so-called Second Revolution (the first was completed when Hitler won the struggle for power by becoming dictator). There remained a vast army of rank-and-file Party members and Storm Troopers who were still poorly rewarded for their contribution to the Nazi victory. Their dissatisfaction made them a danger to Hitler. Hence, not long after becoming Führer, Hitler bluntly warned the SA masses: "I will suppress every attempt to disturb the existing order as ruthlessly as I will deal with the so-called second revolution."[23]

The loudest agitator for a Second Revolution was Röhm, and he was not cowed; it would take a couple of well-placed bullets to do that. He continued to make noises about a Second Revolution: "If he [Hitler] didn't know it before, he knows now that I'll never allow our revolution to fizzle out. . . . [If] he thinks he can squeeze me for his own ends forever, and some fine day throw me on the ash-heap, he's wrong. The S.A. can also be an instrument for checking Hitler himself."[24]

Röhm was not one who could keep his mouth shut or his intentions concealed. Jarman says he acidly complained (a complaint that quickly flew via informers straight to Himmler and Hitler):

"Then, referring to the [congratulatory] New Year letter from Hitler: 'He can't,' said Röhm, 'fool me. . . . Yes, we still need him. Unfortunately, half the nation already sees a demi-god in him. But we must push him soon, lest the others push him first. . . . If Hitler is reasonable, I shall settle the matter quietly; if he isn't, I must be prepared to use force—not for my sake, but for the sake of our revolution.' On 4 June [1934] Hitler spent five hours with Röhm. 'I implored him for the last time,' Hitler reported later, 'to oppose this madness of his own accord,' and to 'use his authority so as to stop a development which in any event could only end in a catastrophe.' But apparently Röhm was neither won over nor intimidated. For the immediate future, Hitler ordered the S.A. on leave for July, and Röhm himself went on sick leave on 7 June [1934]—but not without a message to his men which contained a challenge to the enemies of the S.A.: 'At the hour and in the form which appears to be necessary they will receive the fitting answer.' To Röhm there seemed no immediate danger. Like so many others, he, too, underestimated Hitler."[25]

At the bottom of the heap, the ragtag SA petty clerks and manual laborers, if they had jobs at all (most of the SA were not salaried by the Party before 1933), pressed their noses against a frosty window and watched their betters wolf down goodies in cozy luxury. They generally had no particularly idealistic Socialistic pretensions. They just wanted a slice of the pie. That is what they thought they had fought for, and that is what Röhm thought he would give them through a Second Revolution that would implement the Socialism part of the NSDAP's Socialist ideals, which Röhm foolishly took seriously.

In fact, before Hitler became Chancellor he intended to abolish the Socialism in National Socialism. Former Chancellor Franz von Papen and Hitler met secretly on January 4, 1933, and agreed on a political deal, two of the principal points of which were Hitler's promising to renounce the Socialist part of his program (which is what he meant to do in any event), and Papen's promise to prevail upon President Hindenburg to appoint Hitler Chancellor (which Hindenburg did on January 30, 1933, with much reluctance). Presumably, also part of the deal was that Papen was to become Vice Chancellor, an office he did assume under Hitler. Papen thought he could out-maneuver Hitler and regain executive control of Germany, a grotesque miscalculation on his part.

Papen's motive was also born out of sheer spite. It was a retaliatory move against Schleicher, who had first persuaded Hindenburg to appoint Papen Chancellor and then later about-faced and got Hindenburg to get rid of Papen because Schleicher decided he did not like the color of Papen's politics. Schleicher had done exactly the same thing in the case of Papen's predecessor in the Chancellorship, Heinrich Brüning.

Schleicher, upon appointment by Hindenburg, took over as Chancellor after Papen, and now Papen wanted to topple Schleicher. Some historians say Hitler might never have achieved power had there been no feud between Schleicher and Papen.

Though the NSDAP* was the largest party in Germany at the time, Hitler could not muster enough votes for victory when he ran for President in 1932. Politically, Germany was in turmoil, but the factors of desperation upon which Hitler had built his strength (World War I defeat, the war's terrible aftermath, and the Depression of 1929) were dissipating; recovery of the nation was within sight, and Hitler, with growing alarm, was well aware of the disastrous, possibly terminal effect that would have on his political chances. Thus, the deal with Papen and the eager chucking of the Nazi Party's Socialist program, which was so dear to Röhm's heart.

Except for Röhm and others who shared his politically naive views, Nazis who were soaking up *la dolce vita* could not possibly care less about the deprived Nazi class. Röhm, of course, was not part of the latter. In the upper strata of the Party and SA the view was dazzling. The lifestyle enjoyed by SA Chief of Staff Röhm, his colleagues, and his homosexual buddies, was magnificently opulent—replete with beautifully tailored uniforms sporting those exquisitely crafted, frequently damascus-bladed daggers patterned after the Swiss Mercenary style, a choice suggested by Göring that stemmed from a sixteenth-century Swiss Holbein dagger he had seen in a Munich museum. Also worn were fancily engraved small and compact Walther 7.65mm. automatic pistols, which Hitler christened the Nazi "Weapon of Honor." There abounded splendid apartments, villas, big sleek Mercedes cars and flashy sports cars, and all the other trappings of the richly affluent, including the wherewithal to throw lavish parties on a whim. Röhm and other top-level SA used Party funds for this purpose until the Blood Purge, when Hitler told Röhm's successor, Viktor Lutze, to stop using Party money for unofficial merrymaking.

The SA gay parties were attended by many of Germany's handpicked, crisply handsome males, who were decked out in Nazi uniforms cut of the finest materials and tight-fitting in all the machismo right places. These all-night parties, complete with a small orchestra and smartly liveried waiters, usually turned into drinking and gay-sex sprees—which is what they were intended for

---

*The German term from which this abbreviation originates is *Nationalsozialistische Deutsche Arbeiterpartei*—National Socialist German Workers Party.

in the first place. And Röhm was not at all self-conscious about it. He divided people into friends and enemies, not much giving a damn what his enemies thought of him. In fact, in 1925 he called the police and brought charges against a 17-year-old male prostitute who stole a suitcase of his that contained some love letters—letters which were published in German newspapers as a result of the consequent court suit. Gay love letters were among his most precious possessions, along with his vast collection of gay pornography.

Röhm bemusedly shrugged off flurries of complaints about wild drinking orgies and debauchery, corruption and low behavior, in his immediate circle. However, there were some occasions when he became irritated and expressed indignation. "Those hypocrites!" Röhm once exploded. "I've suffered enough from that. . . . Homosexuality isn't a reason for removing an able and honest leader from any position, so long as he is discreet. [Röhm was definitely *not* discreet.] Such a more or less natural abnormality is nobody's business. . . . Haven't I worked all my life for this land and given Hitler all I had? Where would he be without me? Hitler had better look out—the German revolution is only beginning!"[26]

A humorous footnote to this friction between Hitler and Röhm cropped up in an interview quoting the Führer that appeared in *The New York Times* of March 31, 1934. The two were locked in bitter conflict then and Hitler may already have been thinking about staging the Blood Purge that he was to execute three months later:

"It would be nothing short of an insult to think that any men who have stood with me year after year are being animated by any desire to supplant me.

"The world has never seen a more striking example of unquestioning fidelity than that shown by my associates. The reason, perhaps, why such stories arise lies in the fact that I have associated myself, not with zeros, but with real men. Zeros are round, hence they are the first to begin to roll and tumble when adversity comes.

"The men about me are four-square and upstanding men—each of them a powerful personality, each of them a man with will and ambition. If they had no ambition, they would not be where they are to-day. I welcome ambition. When you have a group of powerful personalities, it is inevitable that occasionally friction is produced.

"But never yet have any men who follow my leadership sought to impose their will upon mine. On the contrary, they have adapted themselves marvellously to my every desire."

Politicians are habitual liars, but in this particular case Hitler's prevarication with regard to Röhm "adapting" himself "marvelously" to Hitler's "every desire" is especially flagrant. In 1934, they were decidedly well into the final shouting-match stage of their relationship. Just about everybody who got a taste of Hitler's bellowing, screaming, wall-and-table-smashing, fist-pounding tantrums (which were half insane and half a product of shrewd calculation—an act) was completely intimidated and shattered by the experience. Not so Röhm. They had come too far, too long, together for Röhm to start quaking before Hitler. They knew each other inside out—except that Röhm did not believe Hitler could go so far as to kill him. Röhm was not the type to cave in to anyone, and certainly not to Adolf, whom Röhm had helped rescue from the gutter and placed upon the path of glory. Hitler was to a quite substantial extent Röhm's protégé, Röhm's virtual creation, as both well knew.

The other most influential person in Hitler's early political career was the alcoholic Dietrich Eckart. He was Hitler's political and spiritual mentor, who taught him how to dress and behave in polite society, and secured for him very valuable connections in social and business circles. Hitler often spoke of Eckart with tears in his eyes. He prominently mentioned Eckart in *Mein Kampf,* but, said Konrad Heiden in his introduction to the book, "never mentions the name of Captain Ernst Röhm, who contributed at least as much as himself [Hitler] to the rise of the party." This must have sorely rankled Röhm upon publication of the first part of the book in 1925. So, when Hitler screamed, Röhm screamed right back—literally and, upon occasion, for hours at a stretch. In fact, their last private meeting shortly before Hitler ordered Röhm executed was a nonstop five-hour shouting marathon.

Almost unquestionably, Hitler must have many times tried through palms-up pleading, and calm rational argument, and roared orders and threats to get Röhm to cool down his orgies to a discreet nonpublic level and to demand that his cohort do likewise. And, of course, there was also that Second Revolution thing, which so infuriated Hitler. For political expediency the former radical had become an arch conservative as Führer. Hitler was aware that a Second Revolution could topple him. The fur flew, but Hitler could neither checkmate Röhm's Socialism nor batten down his and the SA gay faction's unrestrained homosexual amours—short of killing them all, that is.

Hitler's and Röhm's snarling encounters, punctuated by warm hand-clasping misty-eyed reconciliations, were—Röhm felt—just nothing more than a hard-bitten and hard-boiled soldier's way of resolving interpersonal differences between comrades. Both he and Hitler were spawned by the trenches of World War I. Röhm did not give very much serious thought to the homosexual issue; he did not consider it a matter of particular importance in openly gay Germany, and, besides, he viewed sex in general as a more-or-less purely private concern (he was once reported to have barked in a confrontation with a heterosexual moralist, "My private sexual behavior is none of your goddamn business!").

Röhm attached so little import to homosexuality that it seems that nearly everyone except Röhm and most of his WWI heterosexual Army pals knew or suspected that he was gay before Röhm himself became cognizant of it. Konrad Heiden concluded that Röhm first became conscious of his "unfortunate disposition" in 1924.[27] Presumably around this time Röhm wrote a letter to a Dr. Karl-Guenther Heimsoth, a *Freikorps* fighter, early Nazi, and astrologer. He had published a book titled *Charakter Konstellation,* which was devoted entirely to the horoscopes of homosexuals. In the letter to Heimsoth, Röhm said, "You are obviously very skilled at judging horoscopes. Could you not have a look at mine. . . ? Then I might learn what sort of person I am. . . . I suppose that I am homosexual." Heimsoth, a homosexual, was murdered in the Blood Purge because of his connection with Röhm and because he was gay.

Röhm probably knew about his "unfortunate disposition" for some time before 1924; the gay scene was certainly not foreign to him before then. A growing self-awareness of one's homosexual orientation—while it may come late in life and perhaps be preceded by self-denials—is not something one wakes up to one morning and exclaims, "Golly gee! I'm a homosexual!" Hitler had an uncanny ability to immediately size up a person at a first meeting, divining his strengths, weaknesses, capabilities, talents, hopes, fears, and desires, sexual and otherwise. Hitler's ability in this regard is so well proven that it seems that he must have known about Röhm's homosexuality, or incipient homosexuality, from the start of their political career and friendship in 1919.

Whether Röhm was openly gay at that time or not, one cannot refer to Röhm as being in or coming out of the gay closet. He was not the type of man who would or could tolerate any kind of closet. So, in short, it seems fairly safe to assume that sometime between 1919 and 1924 Röhm fully awakened to his preference and thereafter made the most of it. Before then, or during the war, he may or may not have given gay sex a fling; if he did he might have considered it only a lark. Fellow officers who had known Röhm during the war maintained that he had been "normal," and described orgies in which he had taken part in Army brothels. However, many people do not realize that it is not at all unusual for gays to have jolly good times in straight whorehouses. As far as Röhm was concerned, sex was just good clean fun, and Röhm, although a brilliant monster and killer, was decidedly a fun-loving man. This is one of the reasons Hitler found him so appealing in the first place. Hitler tended markedly to be sour, dour, and overserious (except in the company of females); and most people such as he find vivacious personalities very attractive. Röhm was marvelous company to be with—if you were not his enemy.

Hitler's troubles in trying to totally force his will upon Röhm and the SA began to assume massive proportions April 1, 1924. That was the day he gave Röhm full authority to reconstitute the SA after it had been dissolved by Gustav Ritter von Kahr following the Munich beer-hall putsch fiasco of November 8-9, 1923, when Hitler attempted to take over the government by force. (Kahr, State Commissioner of Bavaria, was murdered in revenge by the Nazis in Munich on June 6, 1934. He was hacked to death with an axe.)

In March 1923, Hitler had given Hermann Göring supreme command of the SA, and it was Göring on orders from Hitler who appointed Röhm Deputy Commander of the SA on April 1, 1924, with Gerhard Rossbach (the gay "prophet") being named Chief of Staff. A year later, on May 1, 1925, Röhm quit because of the split with Hitler over the issues of Röhm's desire to militarize the SA and his demand that the SA be made independent of Party-apparatus control. Hitler would tolerate neither. The breach with Röhm lasted five years, during most of which time he was in Bolivia serving as an instructor and adviser on the General Staff of the Bolivian Army as a Lieutenant-Colonel, along with a group of other former German Army officers.

On November 1, 1926, Hitler appointed former Army Captain Franz Pfeffer von Salomon as SA Supreme Leader, and the same war-of-wills fight Hitler had with Röhm broke out all over again with Salomon. He was as refractory as Röhm. Hitler told Salomon that the SA was above all to conduct propaganda. Salomon shot back that he was not in command of a bill-posting column. Hitler and Salomon published successive decrees in the Party's newspaper, the *Völkischer Beobachter,* whereby the one revoked the orders of the other.

Salomon, who loved to play soldier, ordered the SA on cross-country maneuvers—and Hitler forbade them. The statements they made about the purpose and organization of the SA contradicted one another exactly. "The SA is only a defense detachment," swore Hitler. "It is a storm detachment," swore Salomon. Salomon modeled the SA on the Army, which Hitler in livid anger opposed. "I will not undertake the responsibility for your military foolery," shouted Hitler. "I will undertake it," replied Salomon stonily. Salomon recognized Hitler only as a political drumbeater, not as a suitable commander of an SA army strike force. "I refuse to be browbeaten by that flabby Austrian," said Salomon after one of countless heated exchanges between the two.[28]

Hitler needed a personal political-power base in the SA, distinct from the Army or any Army-like status. Even if the German Army had had no objection to absorbing the SA, or being absorbed by it (the Army was vitriolically contemptuous of the SA), Hitler still would have been absolutely against it, including objecting to an SA man, Röhm, becoming Minister of War. (Hitler did make Röhm a Cabinet Minister, but without portfolio.) Obviously, had the SA and the Reichswehr (Army) melded, Hitler would have effectively lost the SA as a power base, which before 1934 was a considerably larger force than the Army because of restrictions that had been placed on the Army by the Treaty of Versailles following Germany's defeat in World War I. Hence, it was during Salomon's chieftainship of the SA, and after Hitler formed the SS in 1925, that he issued emphatic orders forbidding either the SA or the SS to have any connection whatsoever with the Reichswehr. Still, many of Hitler's followers at the time could not get it through their heads that he intended to be the sole master of the Movement. He wanted no "partners," and would not tolerate any, especially Röhm.

On August 29, 1930, Hitler dismissed Salomon and on September 2, 1930, appointed himself Supreme Leader of the SA and SS in a move to make it crystal clear that they—*particularly* the SA—were responsible to him and him alone. Then in the same month, September, he recalled Röhm to reassume the operational reins of the SA, which Röhm did on January 5, 1931, in the position of SA Chief of Staff. Whatever else Hitler felt about Röhm, the Führer saw him as the best choice for the job, his homosexuality notwithstanding.

Röhm's homosexuality was household gossip in Germany long before 1931, so in order to smooth Röhm's path and head off divisive opposition when he resumed the SA post, Hitler issued the following official statement on February 3, 1931:

"The Supreme Command of the SA [Hitler] has considered a number of reports and charges levelled at SA officers and men, most of them embodying accusations in respect of their personal conduct.

"It emerges from an examination of these matters that most of them fall entirely outside the scope of SA service. In many cases, attacks by political or personal opponents have been taken on trust.

"Some people expect SA commanders of high and senior rank to take decisions on these matters, which belong purely to the private domain. I reject this presumption categorically and with all the force at my command.

"Quite apart from the waste of time which could be better employed in the fight for freedom, I am bound to state that the SA is a body of men formed for a specific political purpose. It is not an institute for the moral education of genteel young ladies, but a formation of seasoned fighters. The sole purpose of any inquiry must be to ascertain whether or not the SA officer or other rank is performing his official duties within the SA. His private life cannot be an object of scrutiny unless it conflicts with basic principles of National Socialist ideology."[29]

What mightily disturbed Hitler was that intra-Party name-calling was giving the Movement a bad image and creating a house divided against itself. As an ominous threat added to his February 3, 1931, statement, he warned: In the future it will be "necessary to check whether the author of a denunciation should himself be called to account for sowing discontent among his seasoned fellow-warriors." Take care of Party interests first and all else second, demanded Hitler, in effect, of his anti-gay followers. Gays were anathema to him, too, but political expediency took precedence.

Despite all this brouhaha swirling around Röhm, he was overjoyed to be back in the saddle again. His sojourn in Bolivia had not been a happy one. He was only too glad to oblige Hitler, to return to the beloved homeland, and (try) to make peace with Hitler. Röhm was homesick for the abundance of easy gay sex to be enjoyed in Germany. He had been, says Bleuel, "pleased with his work as a military adviser but tormented by the sexual privations of Bolivia, where 'my favourite form of activity' seemed to be unknown [it was not and is not; it was just very much underground]. The following lament from afar was addressed to a Dr. Heimsoth, who shared his tastes: 'So here I am, poor fool, not knowing what to do with myself. I think back sadly to beautiful Berlin, where a man can be so happy.' He also recalled his correspondent's 'enchantingly lovely collection of [gay porn] pictures' and begged him to forward a few copies."[30]

Some of those plaintive letters from Bolivia were filched and leaked to the press by an unknown informant and published in March 1932. One suspects the hand of the SS in this matter. The SS was then a subordinate organization of the SA, and Himmler was champing at the bit to be shed of Röhm and assume independent power, even though Himmler and his SS, as Hitler's bodyguard force, were more answerable to Hitler than to Röhm. (Interestingly, Himmler wrote in a letter to Röhm on his birthday just a few months before the Purge: "It was, and is still, our greatest pride to be one of your most faithful followers." At the time, Himmler was sharpening his dagger to cut Röhm's and the SA's collective throat.) Around 1932 the SS (Schutzstaffel, or Elite Guard) was a "minor" 50,000-man unit, but one that Hitler trusted far more than the unruly SA. The trust factor was paramount in his mind, which is what motivated him to establish the glacially obedient SS in 1925.* Himmler felt that all his authority derived from Hitler. He was the archetypal yes-man; Röhm was not. Hitler elevated the SS to the status of an independent organization after the Blood Purge; on July 26, 1934, as the reward for carrying out executions of SA men and others, Hitler decreed SS independence. Himmler in his new position as Reichsführer-SS answered to Hitler alone. What the Armed Forces feared in the SA would become a reality in the SS.

With the publication of Röhm's gay letters from Bolivia, there flared a Party squabble that bordered on chaos. Unlike the gay love letters published in 1925 when Röhm was a nobody, Party leaders howled for blood with the publication of the Bolivia letters in 1932 when Röhm was very much of a somebody—the leader of 400,000 Storm Troopers (in 1932), and one of the most prominent figures in the Nazi hierarchy. Röhm at first tried to deny authorship of the letters. He might have better weathered the storm, in view of his bulldoggish, obstinate personality and because he still had Hitler's support, but things had gotten out of control; delaying the inevitable was only making the situation worse.

Regarding this matter, an interesting comment was a July 26, 1932, contemptuous entry in the diary of Helmut Klotz, a key figure in the Weimar national military defense force, whom Röhm met in an attempt to secure Army barracks, maneuvering grounds, and arms for the SA:

"To-day I had a distinguished visitor: Captain Röhm, the so-called 'Chief-of-Staff of the Storm Troopers and Defense Corps.' A painful figure! A few days ago he was the chief participant in a

---

*The SS grew out of the *Stabswache* (Headquarters Guard), Hitler's black-shirted bodyguards formed by him from SA members after the 1923 Beer Hall Putsch. Each young man, some of whom were gay, was personally selected by Hitler, which is what originally gave the incipient SS its distinctive lean and hard and wolfishly menacing appearance and character.

scandalous law case in Munich. A political journalist had published his pederastic correspondence (Röhm is a hundred per cent homosexual of the most disgusting type) months before, and, driven by necessity, the 'Chief-of-Staff' had thereupon responded by laying a charge against him and asserting that the letters were forgeries. His opponent took up the charge and offered to prove his case before the court. For a long time Röhm did his best to postpone the case; but at last the day came. The proceedings were fixed to begin at 9:30. At 9:25 Herr Röhm withdrew his charge and declared himself ready to pay the costs.

"The letters are genuine and Herr Röhm, Hitler's right hand man and better half, is one of the most notorious pederasts walking about on this earth.

"And that was the creature I had to receive to-day! Schleicher advised me to deal with him sitting and not to leave my chair even for a second. 'Then nothing can happen to you. But be on your guard; Herr Röhm is supposed to be very ardent!' "[31]

Hitler tried to quash the whole mess by distributing a leaflet on April 6, 1932, in which he said: "Röhm remains my Chief of Staff both now and after the elections [of 1932]. Nothing will alter this fact, not even the filthiest and most loathsome smear campaign, which does not shrink from falsifications, illegalities and abuses of authority, and which will make due atonement under the law."[32]

Straight Nazis latched onto the incident as a fulcrum to urge Hitler to fire Röhm "because he was filling senior posts in the SA and SS according to his personal [homosexual] inclinations."[33] The uproar over gay jinks was a tempest in a teapot, but a very ugly and embarrassing one. "Normal" Nazis' hue and cry over the issue of homosexuality in the Movement was splintering the Party and fracturing Hitler's control over it. Röhm and the SA were clearly getting out of hand, and homophobic Nazis were mad as hell. The Bolivia letters prompted the future Party kingpin Martin Bormann to write to his boss, Deputy Führer Rudolf Hess:

"I have nothing against Röhm as a person. As far as I'm concerned, a man can fancy elephants in Indo-China and kangaroos in Australia—I couldn't care less. But: It is drummed into every SA man and every ordinary Party member—and this was particularly important in Röhm's case—that he must back his comrades and leaders to the hilt, even when blunders occur. And now the most prominent SA commander goes slandering and denouncing people in this blatant manner. If the Führer hangs on to the man after this business, I can't fathom him any longer. . . ."[34]

Bormann was not so sexually sophisticated as he pretended. This satyr, who was intent on bedding as many women as possible, all with his wife's approval and blessing, was full of bilious loathing for Röhm and what Bormann called the "gang of fairies" around Röhm.

Characteristically, Röhm was not particularly perturbed by attacks on his lifestyle, except to vilify his slanderers, which is what Bormann was referring to in his letter to Hess. Röhm's typical response to such attacks is contained in an Order of the Day distributed to the entire SA and SS after the Nazis gained power. He spelled out his attitude in no uncertain terms:

"I take advantage of the prevalence of these often absurd excrescences of prudishness, and worse, to make it clear that the German Revolution has been won, not by philistines, bigots and sermonizers, but by revolutionary fighters who will secure that revolution and that alone. It is the SA's task, not to keep watch on the attire, complexion and chastity of others, but to haul Germany to its feet by dint of their free and revolutionary fighting spirit.

"I therefore forbid all officers and men of the SA and SS to employ their activities in this field and allow themselves to become the stooges of perverse moral aesthetes. This applies also, and in particular, to those SA and SS officers whom I have appointed to police commissionerships or other government posts: Röhm, Chief of Staff."[35]

The shadeless nature of the man was such that either you were his bosom friend (though, of course, not necessarily sexually) or you were his enemy. He told his enemies to get lost one and all, and continued with great vigor his sybaritic reveling all over Germany and especially in Berlin, where he was frequently seen merrymaking at the Kleist-Kasino and the Silhouette gay bars and sexually luxuriating at the Turkish baths. His banquets and orgies at his Berlin and other headquarters were sumptuous affairs that gays and fun-loving straights eagerly attended. Röhm was the vortex of a gay scene in Germany the likes of which have often been matched but rarely surpassed. In fact, one of the reasons why he retreated to the Hotel Hanslbauer, a health spa at Bad Wiessee in June 1934, where he was arrested by Hitler, was because of a nerve ailment exacerbated by the exhaustion of too much work combined with too much play. Reportedly, he hardly ever awakened each morning without a thundering hangover.

Once Röhm was back in stirrups in 1931 he immediately began to build an entourage of old friends and handsome new faces. He especially wanted Edmund Heines back at his side. Hitler had expelled him from the Party in 1927. Heines was a young man of enormous energy and ability as well as Röhm's occasional sexual bedfellow. Distinguished by a girlish face on the body of a truck driver, Heines was an elegant, suave, and impeccably groomed killer. He liked to shoot his victims in the face with his 7.65mm. Walther automatic or beat them to death with a club.

Röhm wanted his buddy Heines back because he was a loyal, hardworking, exceptionally capable, and fearless man, even though people had to keep from smiling when Heines opened his mouth and spoke. His voice was like that of a soft-purry-sounding, coy, demure young girl. But Heines was no queen, no wilting lily. Behind that feminine feline face, big blue eyes, and crinkly curly short golden hair lay immeasurable ferocity and ruthlessness.

In addition to Heines' value to Röhm as a first-rate adjutant, gifted administrative executive, and aggressive and adroit SA Leader, Heines had a marked talent as procurer for Röhm, garnering the fairest lads in the Fatherland for Röhm's sexual amusement. In short, Heines was not only good friend and lover but indispensable in all other departments of Röhm's life.

Röhm pleaded Heines' case with Hitler, then he argued, and finally threatened Hitler. Either take us both back, Adolf, or it is quits right now, demanded Röhm, in words to that effect. Röhm said he would not resume command of the SA unless Heines were reinstated. Hitler was left with no other choice but to readmit Heines to the SA and Party. Hitler not only had to back down but was constrained at Röhm's behest to send Heines a letter thanking him "heartily for his achievements and service to the cause of National Socialism."[36] Thus Hitler had to eat the words he had spoken at the Hirschbräukeller in Munich in 1927 when he angrily, imperiously, and rhetorically asked, "Am I to let such people [Röhm, Heines, and other homosexuals] reproach me with anything!?"

Is it any wonder that when Hitler's "Tag" came upon arresting Röhm at the Hotel Hanselbauer on June 30, 1934, he would scream at him: "You filthy traitor and pervert!"? The first part of that charge was a lie, and Hitler knew it, and the second half was a fact known to him for at least a decade. Is it any wonder that among the *first* victims of the Blood Purge were Heines and his handsome young SA chauffeur? Hitler found them naked in bed together—the intimation is that they were having sex when Hitler discovered them—that June 30th morning and in spluttering fury ordered that they be taken away and immediately shot. Some reports place the shootings on the grounds outside the Hotel Hanselbauer, in the back seat of an auto.

Is it any wonder that, according to eyewitnesses in the hotel, Hitler ordered forthwith the blanket "ruthless extermination of this pestilential tumor"—that is, of homosexuals?[37] It did not matter that under Röhm's and Heines' helmsmanship the SA had leaped forward to staggering heights of power, strength, and membership: from 100,000 men in 1931 to 400,000 in 1932, and about 3,000,000 in 1933-1934. The SA had also achieved new heights in spreading nationwide terror and free-floating intimidation. All very much to Hitler's liking—before 1933-1934. Six months previously, on January 1, 1934, Hitler wrote Röhm:

"My dear Chief of Staff: The fight of the National Socialist Movement and the National Socialist Revolution were rendered possible for me by the consistent suppression of the Red Terror by the SA. If the army has to guarantee the protection of the nation against the world beyond our frontiers, the task of the SA is to secure the victory of the National Socialist Revolution and the existence of the National Socialist State and the community of our people in the domestic sphere. When I summoned you to your present position, my dear Chief of Staff, the SA was passing through a serious crisis. It is primarily due to your services if after a few years this political instrument could develop that force which enabled me to face the final struggle for power and to succeed in laying low the Marxist opponent.

"At the close of the year of the National Socialist Revolution, therefore, I feel compelled to thank you, my dear Ernst Röhm, for the imperishable services which you have rendered to the National Socialist Movement and the German people, and to assure you how very grateful I am to Fate that I am able to call such men as you my friends and fellow-combatants.

"In true friendship and grateful regard,

Your ADOLF HITLER"[38]

In his book, *Hitler* (page 454), Joachim C. Fest writes that "only a few days after Hitler had thanked his chief of staff and intimate friend in such warm words for his services, the Chancellor ordered Rudolf Diels, chief of the secret state police office (the incipient Gestapo), to gather incriminating documents on 'Herr Röhm and his friendships.... This is the most important assignment you have ever received,' he told Diels."

The strands of the spider's web leading to and culminating in the Purge and gay genocide were spun of these inextricable factors: the homosexual issue plus Röhm's and the SA's drive for independence, military designs, and socialist agitation for a Second Revolution, Röhm's and the SA's general intractability, the SA's boat-rocking rampages of violence and murder (Hitler was concerned about this only insofar as it affected social stability), and sticky layers of intrigues and plots born of the personal ambitions of Hitler's inner circle and other factions.

Doubtless, what finally touched off Hitler's decision to undertake the Purge, and its concomitant crushing of homosexuals once and for all, was a four-minute meeting he had with Hindenburg and Minister of Defense von Blomberg on June 21, 1934. Hitler was flatly told, says John W. Wheeler-Bennett in *The Nemesis of Power,* that if he could not resolve the state of tension between the SA and the Army, and the SA versus the rest of Germany, "the President would declare martial law and hand over the control of affairs to the Army. In the course of a four-minute interview, in von Blomberg's presence, Hindenburg reiterated what the Minister of Defense had already stated, and in less than half an hour after his arrival Hitler found himself on the front steps again in the brilliant pitiless glare of the June sunlight.

"It is probable that Hitler's final decision to suppress the SA by force was taken in the course of his flight back to the Tempelhof on June 21. He could no longer deceive himself. The promise given to the Army with regard to Röhm's legions must be implemented at all costs if the Army was in its turn to honour its share of the bargain. The new tone adopted by von Blomberg, the cold relentless tone of the Prussian officer under direct orders, could have only one meaning—that the support of the Army for Hitler's accession as Chief of State would only be forthcoming if and when the price of that support had been paid in full."[39]

It is possible to believe that there is another reason Hitler hesitated to unleash the Purge against his gay minions: He may have wondered if he could manage it successfully. A bloodletting of this magnitude might have a tendency to cut both ways. The SA was the mightiest force in Germany, a monster created by Hitler. There was a very real possibility that by acting against Röhm and the SA, which supposedly was loyal to Röhm, the monster might turn on Hitler. At the time, the SA was a Praetorian Guard, and Roman history provides many examples of what can happen when such a force feels its own interests jeopardized.

Whatever the case, Hitler had no other option but to strike, and strike hard. Before aged President Hindenburg's death, Hitler needed to deceive the Armed Forces into buying the promise of its independence by his annihilating Röhm and the SA threat. That would give some tangible evidence as well as some eyewash. For all of the cuttingly deprecatory remarks Röhm made about Hitler semiprivately and the volcanic conflict between the two, Röhm was at heart Hitler's man to the bitter end; in his jail cell awaiting execution, Röhm was overheard to murmur over and over, softly, piningly, "*mein Führer, mein Führer, mein Führer,*" as though pending death were a petty matter compared with the loss of his Beloved Führer. Circumstances and the better part of Hitler's wisdom clearly dictated that Röhm must die, and with him all of his personal supporters.

Hitler, however, had absolutely no intention of honoring his promise of independence to the Armed Forces, a promise made aboard the cruiser *Deutschland* about two and a half months before the Purge. On April 11, 1934, Hitler and General Blomberg set out on the *Deutschland* with the Commanders-in-Chief of the Army and Navy to attend spring maneuvers in East Prussia. Hitler offered to suppress Röhm's ambitions and drastically reduce the SA in return for the military's endorsement as Hindenburg's successor as President of the Reich. (The "Pact of the *Deutschland*" could hardly end in anything but a blood purge.) The Armed Forces did not realize that they had been duped. On August 2, 1934, at noon, three hours after Hindenburg breathed his last at 9 A.M., it was announced that the offices of Chancellor and President had been combined in Hitler, and that he had therefore assumed the powers as head of state, with both legislative and executive authority, and also therefore became Supreme Commander-in-Chief of the Armed Forces.

Hitler later that day abolished the title of President, officially assumed the title of Führer, and directed all officers and men of the Armed Forces to swear allegiance to him personally: "I swear by God this sacred oath, that I will render unconditional obedience to Adolf Hitler, the Führer." Thus ended any pretense of Wehrmacht independence. They would have been better off with Röhm. As a matter of fact, Goebbels more-or-less sided with Röhm and his socialist views and vision of an SA People's Army. In a diary entry dated March 27, 1945, Goebbels said:

"I point out to the Führer at length that in 1934 we unfortunately failed to reform the Wehrmacht when we had an opportunity of doing so. What Röhm wanted was, of course, right in itself but in practice it could not be carried through by a homosexual and an anarchist. Had Röhm been an upright solid personality, in all probability some hundred generals rather than some hundred SA leaders would have been shot on 30 June. The whole course of events was profoundly tragic and today we are feeling its effects. In that year the time was ripe to revolutionise the Reichswehr. As things were the Führer was unable to seize the opportunity. It is questionable whether today we can ever make good what we missed doing at that time."[40]

Aside from Hitler's desire and need to satisfy the top brass of the Armed Forces and vituperative homophobes, he saw that the time had now come for the extermination of gays in the Movement and in German life. Grunberger says, "The savage Nazi persecution of homosexuals began during the Röhm Putsch of 30 June

1934. . . ."[41] It was totally in keeping with the "sound feeling of the people," which had become under the Nazis a normative legal concept.

"In truth, Hitler in power no longer needed the S.A. of pre-1933 days. For external violence he needed a professional army; for internal violence a disciplined police corps [SS] that would question no decision of his. The S.A. now embarrassed him," say Lasswell and Lerner in *World Revolutionary Elites.*[42]

To be sure, the SA embarrassed him. In the years preceding the June 1934 Purge, gay sexual behavior knew no bounds. It was flashy and gaudy homosexual harlotry. SA Berlin Leader Karl Ernst, a very good-looking young bisexual, was wont to turn up with many a new SA commander who owed his rank largely to homosexual achievement. Moreover, Heines' raids on the Hitler *Jugend* to enlist handsome youths for the sexual sport of the SA leadership, plus Röhm's orgulous orgies, plus the flaming faggotry of Röhm's Cavaliers, plus the swinging behavior of men of such Teutonic, masculine good looks as Karl Ernst were too much to bear for straight Nazis. To say that Hitler was not personally affected, that he did not care, is ridiculous. Hitler must have been unutterably galled by the brash homosexual "displays" of Röhm, Heines, Ernst, and all the rest of them.

According to John Wheeler-Bennett, the "moral record of the SA was a stench in the nostrils of all decent Germans. Corruption, debauchery and perversion were so openly practised as to be impossible of concealment. The erotic orgies of Röhm himself had long been common knowledge, but it was now established that Edmund Heines, Police President of Breslau, and Röhm's deputy in Silesia, possessed a highly efficient organization throughout the Reich for the explicit recruiting of his male harem. That these conditions existed could not be—and indeed was not—denied, and it was also openly stated in Berlin—and with every justification—that the greater part of the *Winterhilfe* [an annual charity collection to help finance the National Socialist People's Welfare Organization] went into the pockets of the Storm Troop leaders to defray the expenses of the luxurious establishments which many of them had set up.

"These scandals were grist to the mill of the Army's opposition.

Apart from the unsavoury company which they were now called upon to keep by virtue of Röhm's proposals for the amalgamation of the 'Officer Corps' of the SA with that of the *Reichswehr,* it was an added argument that men whose private lives were lived with such obscene publicity were not to be entrusted with the vital business of the Reich's defences. 'Rearmament,' as General von Brauchitsch later remarked, 'was too serious and difficult a business to permit the participation of peculators, drunkards and homosexuals.' "[43]

Because of all this gay whirl, Hitler's July 13, 1934, speech to the Reichstag justifying the Blood Purge as due in large measure to the necessity of "burning out" the "plague-boil of perversion" was not merely a clever device to make the bloodbath palatable to the nation. In that speech, Hitler lied about not knowing the extent to which gays were in command of the SA, but otherwise meant his every word in condemnation of the gay presence in the SA and in German life generally. He really did despise it, and now that the problem of Röhm and the SA had been disposed of he could freely express his true feelings from a position of invulnerability.

Hitler said in that July 13 Reichstag speech that 77 persons had perished in the Purge—61 shot, 13 died "resisting arrest," and 3 committed "suicide." A figure of more than 1,000 was given at the Munich trial in May 1957 in which eyewitnesses and participants in the Purge were heard. But Constantine Fitzgibbon says in *Denazification* that the number killed "was probably some five thousand at least."[44] This figure seems too high, but it would not be surprising if it were in fact an accurate estimate. There was a great deal of unscheduled killing, a lot of it completely contrary to Hitler's wishes (some of the victims were Hitler's cronies). And not the least of it was the precipitate gunning down of suspected and known gays in and out of the SA. On this occasion, homophobe gay-bashers descended wielding not fists or clubs, but pistols.

On orders from Hitler, Röhm was shot in a Stadelheim Prison cell in Munich by two SS officers, Sepp Dietrich and Michael Lippert, on Sunday, July 1, 1934, sometime around noon. The shooting, with pistols, occurred about ten minutes after the SS men offered Röhm a gun with one bullet in the chamber and the option of suicide. Hitler reportedly ordered that Röhm be given that choice. According to various reports, which may or may not be true, but do sound like the man, Röhm told the SS officers he wanted to talk with Hitler. Upon being refused and told to shoot himself, Röhm reportedly said, "If I am to be killed, let Adolf do it himself." Given his ten minutes, in private, the SS men returned and flung open his cell door.

Röhm was standing facing the door. SS warders as an indignity had stripped him to the waist, and he was wearing only the civilian shoes and blue suit pants he had hastily put on upon his arrest; Hitler had forbade him to wear the SA uniform. A shot fired by one SS man hit him in the throat. He crumpled to the floor. The other SS man stepped forward, leaned over, placed the muzzle of his pistol against Röhm's head, and fired once. The bullet penetrated his head and the ceiling of the cell below.

Knickerbocker says, "The nation was stunned [but the Army was pleased]; the Nazi Party itself was partially paralyzed with fear. Hitler had turned his SS (*Schutzstaffel*) Black Guards against his SA (*Sturmabteilung*) Storm Troops, and hundreds of Brown Shirt officers had died before the Black Shirt firing squads, many of them shouting 'Heil Hitler!' as they fell [the action was, they felt, so totally devoid of reason that they assumed they were victims of an anti-Hitler coup d'état]. Most of the members of the Reichstag, that curious gesture of Hitler before democracy, were active or honorary officers in the Storm Troops. A score of seats were empty. Their lawful occupants were dead. The survivors were appalled and not less bewildered than the public. Nobody knew what had happened; what to expect."[45]

After the Purge the Reich Press Office announced: "His [Röhm's] notorious and unfortunate proclivity gradually became such an intolerable burden that the Leader of the Movement and Supreme Commander of the SA [Hitler] was himself forced into the gravest conflicts of conscience."[46] Hans Peter Bleuel says in *Sex and Society in Nazi Germany*, "This was . . . far from the truth. Hitler was wholly indifferent to the homosexual leanings and intrigues of his erstwhile friend and associate."[47]

That quote is a perfect example of the error so many make, a very curious error in view of gay genocide initiated by the Purge. If Hitler did not hate homosexuals, if he did not consider them undesirables, if he did not view them as a threat, if he did not see them as corrupt, corrupters, and a corruption, and without a place in the New Order, then why exterminate them? Hitler was responsible for gay genocide. If he had not willed it, then it would not have occurred. Hitler clearly broadcast both the intention to commit and the act of the extermination of homosexuals in his speech of July 13, 1934.

Moreover, Himmler's position on homosexuals is well known, and is cited elsewhere in this book. Ironically, there is some evidence that the genocide of the Jews was sincerely repugnant to Himmler, and that he would have preferred some other solution—but there is no doubt whatever he heartily approved, sought, and implemented the genocide of gays. However, Himmler did not instigate it. Not until the wind-down of the war would he ever have dared act on his own initiative in any matter of great importance. He was not only Hitler's echo, he cringed in fear of Hitler. A meeting with Hitler would suffuse him with nauseous, stomach-cramping dread and anxiety. (Göring felt somewhat the same. He once said his "heart dropped into his stomach" every time he had to meet with Hitler.)

Hitler was *not* "wholly indifferent" to homosexuality, Röhm's or anyone else's, although he could and did make exceptions. He feared homosexuality, detested it, *and* was fascinated by it. He could be both a pragmatist and a homophobe at the same time. Hitler tolerated Röhm and other gays for years, just as we ourselves tolerate one thing or another for days, weeks, months, or years until the time finally comes when we say—"*No more, that's it.*" Evidence of this is plainly stated in his remarks made on June 30, 1934, after he had arrested Röhm and ordered the summary shooting of Heines, his lover, and others. David Irving supplies Hitler's statement:

"All the SA commanders are now under lock and key except Gruppenführer [Karl] Ernst. I was aware of his [Röhm's?] weaknesses, but I hoped for a long time to be able to channel this affair along the right lines. It's all over now. It's been infinitely hard for me to part from comrades that have fought in this struggle of ours for years on end. These people would have ruined the entire SA. I had to put a stop to it some time.

"The scenes during our swoop on Wiessee were scandalous and shameful—more disgusting than I would ever have thought possible.

"Now I have laid down a clear line: the army is the only bearer of arms. Every man, whether SA or not, is in future at the army's disposal. Any man to whom the Wehrmacht beckons, belongs to it. I have maximum faith in the Wehrmacht and the Reich war minister [Blomberg]. A line has had to be drawn. You can rest assured that I will now establish order."[48]

The "order" Hitler referred to was summed up in a remark addressed to some surviving Storm Troop Leaders at noon on June 30, 1934, in the Munich SA Brownhouse just after the first executions. He declared that for the dead men's corrupt morals alone—i.e., their homosexuality—they deserved to die. Earlier, during Hitler's grisly trip from Wiessee back to Munich—the bullet-holed bloody bodies of Heines and his lover were sprawled in the rear seat of one of the cars in Hitler's convoy, Röhm and other SA men marked for death were under guard in other cars—he made further arrests and ordered further executions. Heiden says in *Der Fuehrer:*

"On his way back, Hitler intercepted car after car full of SA leaders on their way to the conference at Wiessee [a short while previously, Röhm had called a conference to meet at his hotel there; Hitler was scheduled to arrive on June 30, address the SA, and iron out differences between himself, Röhm, and the SA—obviously, what Hitler had in mind was not what Röhm expected]; he ordered some of them to follow him and signified to others that they were arrested—and no attempt to resist was reported. Followed by a long file of dismayed prisoners and frightened henchmen Hitler returned to Munich.

"As Hess later suggested, these arrests were fairly arbitrary, made chiefly on the basis of feeling—and Hitler's feeling seems frequently to have been based on a suspicion that the person concerned had homosexual tendencies. This suspicion, Hess admitted, was not always justified and some of the arrests were the result of 'tragic entanglements,' that is to say, the victims were innocent. In the speech which Hitler made before the non-arrested party leaders at noon on June 30, he chiefly accused Röhm and his men for their loose or depraved conduct and declared that for this alone they deserved to die. To Lutze, whom he had appointed Röhm's successor, he sent an order comprising twelve points, which dealt almost exclusively with parties, drinking bouts, automobile trips, squandering and unnatural lewdness indulged in by Röhm and his gang—and stressed the necessity of putting an end to all that."[49]

The reference to Lutze and the intent of the Twelve Points is summarized here (Lutze had accompanied Hitler to Wiessee): "On the day he [Hitler] arrested Röhm at Wiessee, and even before the latter's murder, he issued Viktor Lutze, the new chief of staff, with an order of the day containing twelve demands addressed to the SA:

" 'I expect all SA leaders to help to preserve and strengthen the SA in its capacity as a pure and cleanly institution. In particular, I should like every mother to be able to allow her son to join the SA, Party and Hitler Youth without fear that he may become morally corrupted in their ranks. I therefore require all SA commanders to take the utmost pains to ensure that offences under Paragraph 175 are met by immediate expulsion of the culprit from the SA and Party. I want to see men as SA commanders, not ludicrous monkeys.' With that, homosexuals were finally declared fair game."[50]

When Hitler told Albert Speer, Reich Architect and later Minister of Armaments and War Production, that the homosexual atmosphere in the SA "nauseated" him, Hitler was not being exactly a hypocrite. When he ordered a "ruthless cleaning out of the plague-boil" of homosexuals, Hitler was not merely seizing a politically opportune expedient. He meant what he said, and meant it with a diabolical vengeance that would soon spread to nearly every homosexual upon whom the civil police, Gestapo, SS, and SD could lay an iron hand.

This, of course, does not mean that June 30, 1934, "turned off" homosexuality as one turns off a spigot, nor, as quoted earlier, was "this odd feature of German life" entirely "driven underground." Naturally, the boys furtively got together. There were a few clandestine gay bars around—some (or all of them) operated *in camera* by the Gestapo and SD in order to get a line on gays—bars in which one put his neck on the chopping block by frequenting them. One unusual example of the post-Purge gay modus vivendi was unwittingly provided by Goebbels himself in 1936. He, as Propaganda Minister, was responsible for the hate campaign directed at gays after the Purge. Heiden says, "They were literally buried in mud. A storm of public defamation descended upon these dead men, which described their unnatural tendencies with the most loathsome details; Goebbels's propaganda made it almost their principal crime that they had defiled the Führer's pure movement with their dirty practices. . . ."[51] Nevertheless, one of Goebbels' soirées turned into what must have been a wild homosexual orgy. The way it came about was this, according to Grunberger:

"Goering, son of a colonial administrator, ex-officer and huntsman, cultivated the company of aristocrats, industrialists and military top brass, while the low-born ex-journalist Goebbels struck a new and socially revolutionary note by patronizing artists and film stars. [This partly accounts for why many homosexual "Aryan" artists and entertainers were protected from the gay Holocaust and exempted from military duty. Their services were often seen as essential for cultural and public morale reasons.] The Führer's two closest henchmen vied with each other in the sumptuousness of their own homes and the displays and receptions arranged under their auspices. Goering's Opera Ball in 1936, for instance, at which guests of honour were drawn impartially from throne-rooms and boardrooms (the ex-Czar Ferdinand of Bulgaria and Krupp von Bohlen, the ex-German Crown Prince and Werner von Siemens), was an ornate junket costing no less than a million marks. Within weeks, Goebbels arranged a nocturnal festival at Peacock Island on the outskirts of Berlin, access to which was afforded by temporary Wehrmacht pontoon bridges. The paths of Peacock Island were lined with torch-bearing page boys in tight-fitting white breeches, white satin blouses with lace cuffs and powdered rococo wigs—drawn from the *corps de ballet* of the state theatres, as well as from the chorus lines of less august establishments in Berlin.

"Since Goebbels's social contacts were less exclusive than Goering's, he had leavened the festive crowd with Nazi stalwarts, but these burly veterans of street fights and tavern brawls were so affected by the rococo setting that they hurled themselves upon the bewigged page boys and pulled them into the bushes. Tables collapsed, torches were dimmed, and in the ensuing fracas a number of Party old fighters and their comely victims had to be rescued from drowning."[52]

For the most part, despite the danger homosexuals faced they still found each other and formed relationships that often must have been dramatically sweet, intense, and bitterly poignant amidst the dark melodrama of those days when the line between life and death was as thin as a razor's edge. It was a time when one knew that he was being hunted, when one knew that he and his lover were on the Extermination List.

Had Röhm not rocked the boat to the point where Hitler had to kill him and hundreds of other Storm Troopers in order to bring the SA to heel, if Röhm had kept the SA in check—if he had been discreet in his own homosexual behavior and demanded the same of his rank and file and gay coterie—there still remains little doubt that homosexuals would not have escaped massacre. Röhm and his cohorts and other gays would have merely occupied for some shorter or longer period the quiet eye of the storm that swept away countless homosexuals throughout Europe.

Herschel Grynszpan, a 17-year-old Polish Jew, at the time of his arrest for the murder of German Embassy Counselor Ernst vom Rath. The shooting, on November 7, 1938, was claimed by the Nazis to be the spark that ignited the "spontaneous" *Kristallnacht* (Crystal Night) pogrom against Jews throughout Germany on the night of November 9, 1938. Grynszpan was to be the object of a spectacular Nazi show trial, but Hitler personally ordered the pending trial dropped when the youth threatened to reveal his love affair with Rath. After that, Grynszpan quietly disappeared into "Night and Fog," probably dying in the slowest and most painful way the Nazis could devise. *(National Archives Photo)*

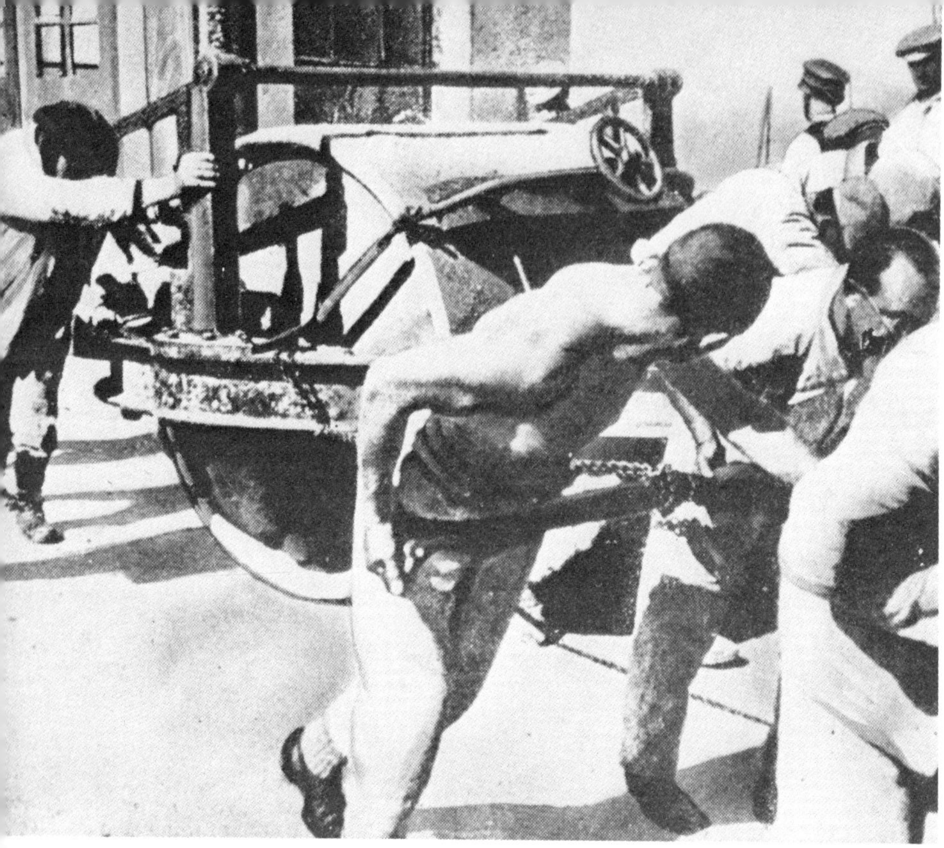

Homosexual prisoners push and pull a road-impaction roller through the dirt streets of Dachau concentration camp from early morning to late evening. Roller detail was normally assigned to Pink Triangles as a form of added punishment because it was one of the worst, most exhausting tasks in camp, and was frequently done under a rain of blows from truncheons and whips along with verbal abuse alluding to homosexuality. The SS and camp kapos took great delight in this torment. *(National Archives Photo)*

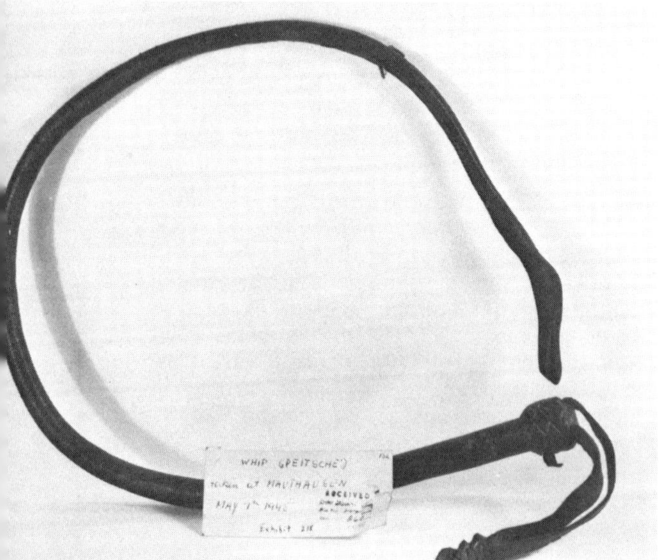

This type of whip, seized at Mathausen concentration camp, was used by the SS and kapos on inmates there and at all other camps and prisons, along with assorted wood clubs, iron rods, rubber truncheons, and testicle crushers (the testicle crushers were centrally manufactured by the SS). A whip like the one shown was found among the belongings of Auschwitz Commandant Rudolf Höss when he was captured. His captors used it on him, to give him a taste of his own whip, although Höss claimed he never whipped or struck a prisoner, and, indeed, never even carried his whip while "working." His whip, he said, was a gift from his wife. *(National Archives Photo)*

A "mild" example of Nazi treatment. The sexual orientation of this prisoner is not known, but it is a sample of how gays were often treated. This man was an inmate at Germany's Waldheim Prison for twelve years. He displays handcuffs he was forced to wear through his entire incarceration. *(U.S. Army Photo)*

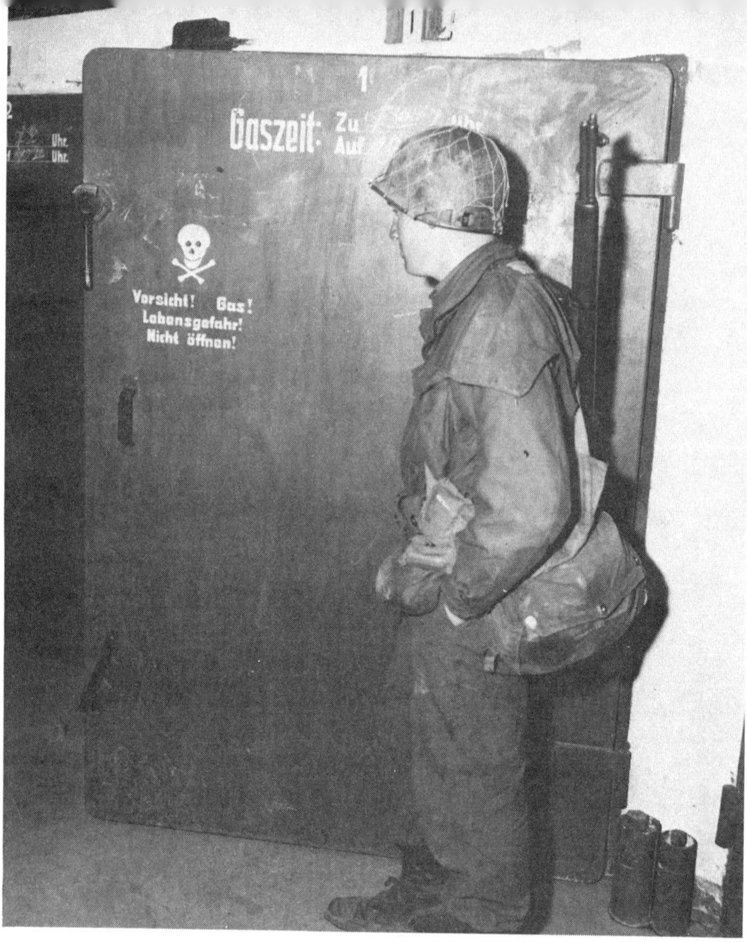

The final solution to the homosexual problem lay behind that door for homosexuals not exterminated in many other various ways. This chamber is at Dachau. The screaming, the weeping, the futile gasping for breath, the agony that room held in air-tight horror was, in its hideous way, a blessing for many gays. It reduced their suffering to about fifteen minutes. *(U.S. Army Photo)*

A can of Zyklon-B, originally intended for use in Czechoslovakia. Tons of the poison were shipped to concentration camps all over Nazi-controlled Europe. Killing-time for a chamber-full of people (250 to 3,000 persons) varied from a matter of seconds to about fifteen minutes. "We knew they were dead when the screaming stopped," said Rudolf Höss, Commandant of Auschwitz. One remarkable SS officer, Kurt Gerstein, requested that the excruciatingly painful irritant placed in Zyklon-B, admixed to alert seepage to manufacturers and handlers, be eliminated on "humanitarian" ground. The request was denied by SS headquarters in Berlin. *(National Archives Photo)*

This is a "luxury" prison at Wuppertal, Germany, and shows gays, political prisoners, and others shortly before the takeover by the U.S. Army in May 1945. Not shown are the rooms with meathooks from which prisoners were suspended and tortured and hanged. In many jails at the close of World War II, SS squads herded the inmates into the prison courtyards and machinegunned them. *(U.S. Army Photo)*

A distinguished group of American journalists visits Dachau. Represented are publishers, editors, and reporters from the *Los Angeles Times, New York Times, Houston Chronicle, This Week Magazine, Chicago Sun, Colliers Magazine,* and the *New Orleans Times*. Represented among the dead—in this case slave laborers deliberately worked to death as one means of extermination—are many homosexuals incarcerated as such—as Pink Triangles, a fact that was common knowledge at the time in Dachau and elsewhere but mentioned only as a "footnote," or not mentioned at all, by that distinguished group of journalists. *(U.S. Army Photo)*

A Dachau "waiting room," called a *Leichenkeller* (corpse cellar for the storage of bodies pending cremation). Dachau, the first Nazi concentration camp, was one of the principle camps in which gays were interned. In this one blood-soaked room (there were many other such sites at Dachau) are piled hundreds of victims, including gays, who awaited cremation when the U.S. Seventh Army liberated the camp in April 1945. *(U.S. Army Photo)*

A *Leichenkeller* at Dachau. In this room are the corpses of gays and others awaiting the furnace. They are mostly young men in their teens, 20s, and 30s. Countless gays, unwilling to bear any longer the torture, beatings, medical experimentation, and starvation, came to the "waiting rooms" as suicides. Many homosexual lovers committed suicide together, while holding hands. *(U.S. Army Photo)*

6

Gay Genocide

About a year before the Purge, on a lovely spring night in Berlin, May 10, 1933, gay genocide was ominously presaged in the smoke and fire of thousands of books and other material that had been set ablaze by hordes of students, SS, SA, and Hitler Youths in the square in front of the University of Berlin. With wild-eyed, sweaty, gleeful abandon, they hurled into the inferno materials seized from various depositories and from Magnus Hirschfeld's world-famous Institute of Sexual Science in Berlin. (Hirschfeld was out of the country on a lecture tour and he wisely never returned to Germany.) It was the Nazis' first large-scale book auto-da-fé demonstration. It followed a May 6, 1933, Berlin newspaper announcement that the city was to be purged of un-German spirit by destroying objectionable books.

Hirschfeld's Institute was a prime focus of that demonstration because Hirschfeld was a Jew, a transvestite, a homosexual, a liberal, a leftist, and, of course, anti-Fascist—all thoroughly unacceptable to the straight Nazi German mentality. (He was once beaten almost to death by Nazis on a street in Munich. He was so badly mauled that the Nazis left him for dead, and a Munich newspaper ran his obituary.) His Institute was described by Nazis as an international center of the homosexual white-slave trade, and an unparalleled breeding ground of dirt and filth. About 12,000 books and much of a unique collection of 35,000 pictures taken from the Institute went up in flames that night. The *Brown Book of the Hitler Terror* records these scenes:

"An attempt was made [at the Hirschfeld Institute] to remove for safe-keeping some of the most valuable private books and manuscripts; but this proved impossible, as the person removing the books was arrested. . . . At 9:30 A.M. some lorries drew up in front of the Institute with about one hundred students and a brass band. They drew up in military formation in front of the Institute, and then marched into the building with their band playing. As the office was not yet open, there was no responsible person there; there were only a few women and one man. The students demanded entrance to every room, and broke in the doors of those which were closed, including the office of the World League for Sexual Reform. When they found that there was not much to be had in the lower rooms, they made their way up to the first floor, where they emptied the ink bottles over manuscripts and carpets and then made for the book-cases. They took away whatever they thought not completely unobjectionable, working for the most part on the basis of the so-called 'black list'. . . .

"The staff was kept under observation during the whole of the proceedings, and the band played throughout, so that a large crowd of inquisitive people gathered outside. At 12 o'clock the leader made a long speech, singing a particularly vulgar song and also the Horst-Wessel song.

"At 3 o'clock a number of truckloads of storm troopers showed up and announced that they were going to continue the work begun that morning. The second troop then proceeded to make a careful search through every room, taking down to the lorries basket after basket of valuable books and manuscripts—two lorry-loads in all. . . . Many bound volumes of periodicals were also taken . . . [and] it did not prove possible to dissuade them from removing the material belonging to the World League for Sexual Reform, the whole edition of the journal *Sexus,* and the card index. In addition, a great many manuscripts, including many unpublished ones, fell into their hands."[1]

There is little doubt Nazi gays were involved in that action. Possibly many homosexuals viewed the destruction of Hirschfeld's Institute as an anti-Semitic act rather than as an expression of anti-homosexual sentiment. Moreover, Hirschfeld's reform efforts had long been disparaged by many gays. In addition, some gays may have been reconciled by the knowledge that Hitler's right-hand man, Ernst Röhm, was a homosexual. "At the outset of the Third Reich, it was all too easy to ignore the clear pronouncements on homosexuality which the Nazi Party had issued," says James Steakley.[2]

One of those "clear pronouncements" was issued by the Party's headquarters in Munich. In 1928, all German political parties were canvassed by Adolf Brand, a gay activist for penal reform generally and reform of Paragraph 175 in particular, the law criminalizing homosexuals and homosexual acts. (Reform was approved in government committee vote on October 16, 1929, but never adopted by the Reichstag because the 1929 Depression crisis took precedence, and the reform measure passed into limbo. The Communist Party, oddly enough, during the committee debate voted *for* reform.) The views of the Nazi Party on Paragraph 175 were emphatically expressed:

"*Community Before the Individual!* Munich, 14 May 1928.

"It is not necessary that you and I live, but it is necessary that the German people live. And it can only live if it can fight, for life means fighting. And it can only fight if it maintains its masculinity. It can only maintain its masculinity if it exercises discipline, especially in matters of love. Free love and deviance are undisciplined. Therefore we reject you, as we reject anything which hurts our people.

"Anyone who even thinks of homosexual love is our enemy. We reject anything which emasculates our people and makes it a plaything for our enemies, for we know that life is a fight and it's madness to think that men will ever embrace fraternally. Natural history teaches us the opposite. Might makes right. And the stronger will always win over the weak. Let's see to it that we once again become the strong! But this we can only do in one way—the German people must once again learn how to exercise discipline. We therefore reject any form of lewdness, especially homosexuality, because it robs us of our last chance to free our people from the bondage which now enslaves it."[3]

One would think that that pronunciamento on the homosexual question by Party headquarters would have been enough to alert gay Nazis to the threat they faced as gays. But they were living in a dream world, as were many others. In 1935 Stefan Lorant said, "They are living in a dream. Their awakening will be a terrible one."[4] Perhaps Nazi gays thought that by hitching their wagons to Röhm's star they would not only remain safe but become helmsmen of the Party and the Reich. This is what Knickerbocker meant when he said that Röhm intended to establish a homosexual government.

Lorant, incidentally, was arrested "on suspicion of Bolshevist intrigue" (a false charge) while editor of the *Münchner Illustrierte Presse,* a nonpolitical illustrated paper. He was thrown into a Munich police prison in March 1933. There he met a 65-year-old farmer who had been arrested for talking about Röhm in a pub: " 'All he likes is young lads. . . . That's all I said,' " complained the farmer. " 'Well, next day they came for me . . . just because I said that about Röhm—that all he likes is young lads. Well, doesn't everyone know that?' "[5]

Hitler was publicly closemouthed about SA gaydom until June 30, 1934, although the Party was not. The Party's campaign against homosexuality began in 1933. Like everything else, it was undertaken on a grand scale. Propaganda films were distributed at discreet intervals, youth leaders were supplied with prepared speeches on the subject, decrees were issued, and repressive measures were taken by the Party. The campaign was based on the precept of "wholesome popular sentiment," of which there are few sentiments more inhuman than the righteous indignation of the frustrated petty bourgeois who gives free rein to his outraged and virtuous sense of propriety. On this plane, the so-called decent average German unhesitatingly identified himself with any government measure, however draconian and illegal. The Nazis actually wrote "wholesome popular sentiment" into the civil penal code as a supplement in a 1935 decree. And the SS weekly, *Das Schwarze Korps,* used banner headlines to brand homosexuals as enemies of the State, and called for their extermination.

Despite the numbers of gays in the Party and Movement, Nazism was and remained heterosexual—straight boy blue and straight girl pink. Amazingly, many Nazi gays must have known that long before 1933 and the advent of the Third Reich the official policy of the Party was unambiguously anti-homosexual. However, unlike many Jews who for a decade before 1933 saw the prospect of disaster growing apace with the Nazi menace and did little or nothing about it, gays were in mid-1934 more-or-less caught with their pants down. When they finally, fully, and hopelessly became aware of their impending doom, it was too late.

After the June 30, 1934, butchery was over, and the bodies of Röhm, his pals, and hundreds of others were hauled away, some in tin-lined slaughterhouse crates, to be burned or discreetly buried, Hitler cleverly used Röhm's homosexuality as a device to defuse a potentially explosive after-shock danger to himself and Party unity. It was far more effective to defame Röhm as a homosexual—everyone knew about that—than it was to try to discredit him as a traitor to the Movement. In fact, Party idealists thought Röhm's agitation for a National Socialist Reich was fully in keeping with Party ideology.

Many SA men, despite their being homophobic, were nevertheless stunned, outraged, and frightened by the Blood Purge. Straight Storm Troopers, along with other straight Nazi adherents, had also been gunned down in the Purge because the object had been not only to remove Röhm and his dedicated gay coistrels but to break the back of the SA and eliminate all real or imagined opposition to Hitler's supremacy. Thus, the mood swirling around Hitler was at first dark and ugly after the initial shock of the Purge had worn off. In fact, many SA gays who escaped being murdered, including nonhomophobic straights loyal to Röhm and his concept of National Socialism and the SA's future role in the life of Germany, retaliated. SS men who pulled the triggers in the Blood Purge kept turning up full of bullet holes, with a bloodstained note pinned to their black tunics that read, "Röhm's Avengers." At least 155 SS leaders were murdered in retaliation by Röhm's faithful in the last half of 1934 and early 1935.

Hitler adroitly nipped possible SA revolt in the bud. His Kroll speech about the Purge delivered on July 13, 1934, made it seem as if homosexuals and traitors were almost one and the same, and that good Nazi straights had nothing to fear. His speech was greeted with blissful sighs of relief, and he turned a pending storm into stormy applause for saving Germany from degenerate traitors. It was a ruthless and brutal act, but Hitler had always told them he was ruthless and brutal, and Germans loved him for it.

After the Purge the fate of gays in Germany and its occupied territories becomes hazy, sketchy, elusive. The Simon Wiesenthal Center for Holocaust Studies, at Yeshiva University of Los Angeles, reports: "One of the major problems of the Nazis' treatment of homosexuals is the lack of authentically documented material on the subject."

Wolfgang Harthauser asserts in his book, *The Great Taboo,* that the historian who wants to treat the theme of the persecution of homosexuals comes up against unimaginable difficulties. Knowledge is mostly a process of accretion, and there are precious few blazed trails to follow that deal with the Nazi evolvement of gay genocide. Those that do exist are often questionable, unreliable, or peter out after a short distance. Extant primary source material is scanty and usually inadequate. Moreover, pertinent records were largely destroyed by the Nazis or in the ravages of war. Also, attempts to secure the cooperation of straight and gay Germans and German organizations have not been very productive. (For example, a German professor of sociology and philosophy who has contact with gay victims of the Nazis flatly refused to cooperate in this study in any way.)

Most discouraging of all is that those who know the most, the surviving "Pink Triangle" victims themselves, have locked away that period of terror in their lives—nearly all of them have thrown away the key. ("Pink Triangle" refers to the triangular pink cloth patch gays were required to wear in concentration camps.) They find reviving those memories too unbearably painful. Also, they feel agonizingly dirtied by that episode in their lives, not because of their homosexuality but because when a person's spirit is cruelly befouled he tends to introject—to turn inward upon himself—all the guilt and shame that should have been felt by the criminal, not by the victim. Rape of the soul is profoundly damaging.

Aside from the emotional trauma involved, talking about their experiences also frequently intensifies debilitary physical reactions. William G. Niederland, clinical professor emeritus of psychiatry at the State University of New York Down-State Medical Center, says: "In my clinical work with concentration camp survivors over the past 30 years I have observed a series of lasting health disturbances which I have described in the professional literature as the survivor syndrome. Among other symptoms, this syndrome includes intense adverse physical and emotional reactions. These reactions manifest themselves not only in nightmares, anxiety dreams, increased tension states, fears of renewed persecution and other emotional disturbances but also in physical conditions of a potentially serious nature, such as hypertension, tachycardia, gastrointestinal disorders, etc."

The terrible wounds to a Pink Triangle's psyche are still raw, and will always be so until the day he takes them to his grave. Pink Triangle survivors are doing just that—they are old, getting older, and dying. They are being swept away like withered autumn leaves in a cold wind.

On top of all the other problems confounding and obstructing research is that *homosexual* is still a dirty word to most people, despite all the pseudosophistication about homosexuality. Being gay is not nice. In West Germany, Paragraph 175 and 175A, the Nazi 1935 revision of the ancient Paragraph 175 German law proscribing homosexual acts, remained in force up until June 1969, when much of Paragraph 175 and all of 175A were abolished. Nevertheless, while Jews and most other victims of the Holocaust have received or been declared eligible for restitution from the West German government, its courts ruled that Pink Triangles were civil criminals under the Nazis and therefore not entitled to restitution. In effect, this means that present-day Germany, along with apparently the rest of the straight world, does not consider the Nazi killings of homosexuals a crime against humanity that merits legal recognition and reparation.

In East Germany, Nazi anti-gay laws were stricken from the statute books immediately after World War II. Unlike pretentiously legalistically minded Nazis, Communists usually do not feel any need for laws for the persecution of gays or anyone else—the laws were abolished there to get rid of the Nazi heritage. The fate of gays in East Germany is believed to be about as bad as it is in Russia, where homosexuality is a crime punishable by up to five years' imprisonment, which turns into a life sentence of personal ruin.

The belated removal of the anti-homosexual law from West Germany's penal code did not remove prejudice and hate from the hearts of the straight majority. Thus, only gays who feel they have nothing to lose, or those compelled by principle (or those of a "perverse" ego) come out of the closet. The rest—about 99 percent—keep their closet doors shut and bolted as tight as a gas chamber door. Gay victims of the Hitler era have no reason to trust anyone.

Another factor militating against disinterring the full story is the legal status of those Pink Triangles who have emigrated from Europe. Their new citizenship was gained under false pretenses by virtue of the concealment of their homosexuality. In the years before, during, and after World War II, visitation or immigration admission was generally denied throughout the world to known or suspected homosexuals. At this writing, America frequently exercises an Immigration and Naturalization Service (INS) regulation to bar or restrict entry for visitation or immigration to known or suspected homosexuals, even though, according to a report in the August 15, 1979, *New York Times,* the U.S. Surgeon General issued an order on August 2, 1979, directing medical officers of the Public Health Service to stop examining and certifying for deportation persons detained by the INS who are known or suspected male or female homosexuals. Presently, such persons seeking to enter the United States may be "paroled" pending examination of their case, but will not be allowed to stay in America indefinitely. Gays who fled Nazi Europe, or left after World War II and took up residence elsewhere, rightly or wrongly fear that their citizenship could be jeopardized if their homosexuality is discovered. Hence, they are closemouthed about their past. Usually, not even ironclad guarantees of anonymity will lure them into telling their story or involving themselves in any way.

What we know about the fate of gays in the Third Reich and elsewhere must be stitched together from bits and pieces of the meager scraps of information available. (What the Nazis did to gays outside Germany is so difficult to ascertain that no attempt has been made to broach the subject in this book.) However, there are cases exemplifying what was not done *for* homosexuals. One of the most noted examples of this occurred in Denmark. Its resistance to Nazism resulted in the sparing of the lives of almost all Danish Jews by foiling the Nazis' attempts to ship them to death centers. According to an Op-Ed page article by Ira Glasser, Executive Director of the New York Civil Liberties Union, in the September 10 1975, issue of *The New York Times,* "The Danish resistance was perhaps best symbolized by the reported willingness of King Christian X to appear in public wearing a yellow Star of David as a sign of fellowship with the persecuted [Jewish] minority. Yet while this brave stand was being made to save the Jews of Denmark, another segment of the population was systematically hunted down and sent to the death camps: Denmark's homosexuals. And Denmark was not unique. Many thousands of German, French, Polish, Hungarian and other European homosexuals were also interned and executed. . . . Many know about the yellow star, but the pink triangle still lies buried as a virtual historical secret. . . . During World War II, no king, no premier, no president, no prominent citizen came forward wearing a pink triangle, as it is said the yellow Star of David was worn by the King of Denmark."

Glasser's remark that the pink triangle still lies buried as a virtual historical secret is indeed true. Steakley, an American university Germanic scholar, says in *The Homosexual Emancipation Movement in Germany:* "Appallingly little information is available on the situation of homosexuals in Nazi Germany. . . . The fact that homosexuals were major victims of Nazism is mentioned in only a few of the standard histories of the period, and those historians who do mention the facts seem reluctant to dwell on the subject and turn quickly to the fate of other minorities in Nazi Germany. Yet tens, perhaps hundreds, of thousands of homosexuals were interned in Nazi concentration camps. They were consigned to the lowest position in the camp hierarchy and, subjected to abuse by both guards and fellow prisoners, most of them perished. The few who managed to survive have been reluctant to reveal their experiences, largely because Paragraph 175 remained on the law books in West Germany.

"The . . . exact number [of homosexuals exterminated during the Third Reich] is unknown and will remain so. Although statistics are available on the number of men brought to trial and convicted on violations of Paragraph 175 during these years [1933-1945], many more were sent to camps without the benefit of a trial. Moreover, many homosexuals were summarily executed by firing squads; this was particularly the case with homosexuals in the military. . . . Finally, many concentration camps systematically destroyed their records when it became apparent that German defeat was imminent."[6]

Hitler's July 13, 1934, speech and the Führer Decree of October 1939 ordered Himmler "to eliminate the harmful influence of such alien parts of the population which represent a danger to the Reich and German folk community." Point 18 of the Party Program further demanded "ruthless prosecution of those whose activities are injurious to the common interest. Sordid criminals against the nation . . . must be punished with death, whatever their creed or race." Finally, there was Hitler's "Order for the Destruction of Lives Which Are Unworthy of Being Lived" (this also included the Euthanasia Program in which about 100,000 German "useless feeders" were put to death in hospitals, sanatoriums, and the like), plus a few other similar edicts, statements, and measures. Apart from the foregoing, there is no known documentation further establishing (aside from the Führer Decree regarding gays in the SS and police) that Hitler ordered the destruction of male homosexuals. (As in the apocryphal story about Queen Victoria, he did not take lesbians seriously.) For that matter, there is no known primary documentation that he ordered the destruction of the Jews.

There was, of course, the Wannsee Conference on January 20, 1942, initiating "the final solution of the Jewish question," and there is no doubt who ordered Göring in July 1941 to order SD Chief Reinhard Heydrich to chair that meeting—Adolf Hitler. ("Unofficially," the order for the gassing of Jews was issued by Himmler in May 1941.) Although there is no evidence that a comparable Wannsee Conference regarding the "Final Solution" of the homosexual question was held, this does not mean one was not convened. In any case, the climate of anti-homosexual prejudice was such that gays were marked for death long before the

Wannsee Conference regarding the Jews was held in 1942. What we know is this: Homosexuals under the Nazis were incarcerated, used as slave labor, and perished through maltreatment or murder. The only concrete difference between the treatment of Jews at the hands of the Nazis and that of homosexuals is solely one of number.

The number of homosexuals killed by the Nazis will never be known; the estimates range from about 10,000 or less to more than 1,000,000. A figure of 220,000 homosexuals killed is often cited in Gay Liberation circles. James D. Steakley says in his *The Homosexual Emancipation Movement in Germany:* "The Protestant Church of Austria recently estimated that 220,000 homosexuals were killed during the Third Reich." Steakley gives as his source for this estimate a report in the November 1974 *Gay Liberator.* The Evangelical Church of the Augsburg Confession in Vienna, Austria, had a "guesstimate" compilation dated January 28, 1978, done for it by one of the Church's pastors at the request of its Bishop Oskar Sakrausky. This report gives an estimate considerably less than 220,000; the figure furnished to Bishop Sakrausky is not quoted here because the basis of its calculation is faulty and includes homosexual civil convictions for the last years of the Weimar Republic.

No estimate of the total number of homosexuals incarcerated and exterminated can be accepted as being more or less accurate than another, unless a figure quoted is suspect or untenable because the source is unproven, otherwise questionable, or invalid. There is no point in citing sources and figures that fall in the latter category. A recent book, *Seminar: Gesellschaft und Homosexualität,* in its chapter about the Pink Triangles states that there were only about 10,000 gay victims. That figure cannot possibly reflect the truth. The book is mentioned because it illustrates the need to be circumspect about statements made by so-called authorities and experts.

Moreover, many of Germany's academicians and others who speak, write, and teach about the Holocaust are the very ones who perpetrated it. In 1968 Wellington Long reported that German prosecution of Nazi criminals at large in that country opened a Pandora's box "to reveal that hundreds of West Germans, including many holding positions of great responsibility and trust, actually were former members of Hitler's murder squads who never had been called to account."[7]

At the sites of the Nazi concentration camps there is little or no indication that gays perished in them. At the Germans' first concentration camp, Dachau, now operated as a memorial and museum, there is no informational material available regarding the thousands of gays who died in that camp, which was used as a principal Nazi medical experimentation center. Gays truly went up in smoke.

Most original written evidence of concentration camp deaths was destroyed by the Nazis. Auschwitz Commandant Rudolf Höss says: "In accordance with orders given by the Reichsführer SS [Himmler] . . . all evidence in Auschwitz on which a calculation of the number of victims might be based had to be burned. . . . I personally destroyed every bit of evidence which could be found in my office. The heads of other offices did the same. [In June 1942 a special unit was assigned to destroy all records of the Holocaust.] According to . . . [Adolf Eichmann, an administrative coordinator for the final solution of the Jewish question], the Reichsführer SS and the Reich Security Head Office also had all their data destroyed. . . . [Eichmann kept a rather precise mental tally of the number of Jews killed and made periodic reports to Himmler. Eichmann apparently was not especially interested in other categories of victims.] Figures given by former prisoners are figments of the imagination and lack any foundation."[8] Even Höss did not know the total number of victims who perished inside (or outside) the camps. Hitler's general policy was that no one was to know more than what was absolutely necessary for him to know to do his job. When questioned after the war, Höss could make only a very rough estimate of total executions in Auschwitz, 2,500,000; this figure does not include 500,000 who perished in ways other than execution.

Although Himmler ordered mass exterminations halted in October 1944, wholesale random killings did not stop until German prisons were taken over and the concentration camps liberated by the Allies in the months preceding Germany's surrender in May 1945. For months after this date, unnumbered thousands died from the effects of disease, starvation, and maltreatment suffered while in the camps and prisons. There were also countless inmates who committed suicide after Germany had been defeated because their lives had been smashed and their families and friends and lovers had gone up in flames. There was no longer anything left to live for.

The question of how many Nazi victims were homosexual is unanswerable. We know the Nazis were deadly intent on removing homosexuals from their own and other societies. In view of their proven ability to root out "undesirables," we begin to perceive that the number of gay Holocaust victims is substantial. If the Nazis eliminated, say, *only 5 percent* of *only* "bona fide" gays *only* in Germany, the victim count might total about 100,000 homosexuals done to death. This figure is based on the March 4, 1937, edition of the SS weekly newspaper, *Das Schwarze Korps* (The Black Corps), reporting that there were 2,000,000 homosexuals in Germany, which was probably an underestimation in view of Kinsey's 1948 publication of his findings on male sexual behavior in America.

Das Schwarze Korps vehemently called for the total extermination of all homosexuals. This was no ordinary editorializing blast. *Das Schwarze Korps* was the organ of the SS High Command, on whose every word Himmler ruled in every edition. Besides his homophobia, he was fanatically concerned about Germany's declining birth rate, which began in the 1920s and extended into the late 1930s; an hysterical obsession probably shared by Hitler. It was compounded by the hundreds of thousands of German males killed in World War I. Females counted for little in Nazi ideology except for their vital function as baby-producing machines and their role as kitchen-, hearth-, and children-tenders. Nazis were sexists and unconcerned about lesbians. Besides, lesbians could and did produce obligatory children for the Fatherland, while most male gays did not.

For a stark comparison of the Nazi's capacity for murder, the aforementioned 5-percent homosexual kill ratio is a low estimate. According to Joseph Tenenbaum in *Race and Reich: The Story of an Epoch,* the Nazis liquidated 73.4 percent of European Jewry plus the Jews killed in Russia.

Morally, it does not matter whether one person or one million perished because of homophobia. However, in terms of historical significance, the number of gays who were murdered is relevant and important. It seems reasonable to conclude that at least 500,000 gays died in the Holocaust because of anti-homosexual prejudice that consequently led to a Nazi policy of gay genocide, however loosely formulated or inconsistent that policy might or might not have been.

Actually, 500,000 may be too conservative a figure. Through torture, gay informers (just as there were Jewish informers), a spy network, and other ways and means, the roundup of gays probably proceeded for awhile at a pace approaching geometric progression; that is, each arrest might lead to about five additional arrests, five could lead to twenty-five, and so on. In the Nazi domain, as in a jungle, one might be able to hide for awhile, but there is virtually no place to run. On February 28, 1933, a month after Hitler was named Chancellor, the "Decree for the Protection of the People and the State" set forth that "Articles 114, 115, 117, 118, 123, 124 and 153 of the constitution of the German Reich are to be suspended until further notice. Consequently, restrictions of personal liberty, of the right of free expression of opinion, including freedom of the press, of association, and of assembly, interference with letters, mail, telegraph, and telephone secrets, orders to search houses and to confiscate as well as restrict property beyond existing legal limits are permissible."[9] That night, February 28, more than 10,000 arrests were made throughout Germany.

On July 6th of the same year Hitler was legitimately able to boast to the Reich Commissioners in the Reich Chancery in Berlin: "We now have absolutely the power to enforce our will everywhere."[10] For gays, the long arm of Nazi terror was indeed *everywhere*. There were few ways to escape. In the early years, gays who had lovers or friends in the SA, SS, Gestapo, and in other influential circles of the Nazi network were often able with their help to evade dragnets or slip out of the country, but this became more and more difficult with the passage of time and the mounting fury of the Nazi murder machinery.

Any attempt to arrive at an accurate estimate of the total number of gays killed is frustrated, too, because thousands of heterosexuals were maliciously or mistakenly accused of being homosexual. They were branded with the pink triangle and died alongside the homosexuals those straights hated so much. Himmler once asked his physiotherapist, Felix Kersten, to act as a consultant on homosexual matters. Kersten was shocked and frightened by the proposal. It was one thing, for example, to be a documented "Aryan" serving as an adviser on Jewish questions because there was little chance of someone labeling the adviser a Jew. However, this was not the case in the homosexual area.

Kersten said to Himmler: "You know yourself that ever since it was known how severely you were dealing with homosexuals it has become a source of the most malicious denunciations. In earlier days if you wanted to get rid of anyone you said they were a witch or in league with the devil. Today you accuse them of homosexuality and proceedings are set in motion. I will have nothing to do with it, not even as a doctor."[11] As Himmler's physician, Kersten could get away with back-talk. The dénouement is ironic when one considers that before falsely accused straights died they were subjected to the same murderous abuse and rapes inflicted on gays. The straights' pleas of sexual normalcy were met with derisive laughter and obscenities before, during, and after being assaulted.

In sum, it is academic to raise the question of whether or not there is proof of either a "Führer Order" or a codified program to kill male gays in Germany and the occupied territories. Himmler, the helmsman of the apparatus of death, sought and implemented a final solution of the homosexual problem. Thousands of gays were sent to civil prisons, but more thousands were shipped directly to concentration camps. Thus, for gays, all roads led to death. In the *Konzentrationslager,* gay genocide took place, with or without an express directive to stamp out the "disease" of homosexuality.

Waite says, "The life of a prisoner counted for nothing. Prisoners disliked by the guards [gays were a primary target] were arbitrarily selected for injections, . . . which means they were murdered through injections of Phenol or Evipan, only one of a number of methods of killing. Prisoners were often trampled to death with nailed boots, or drowned in cesspools, or driven into the electrically charged barbed-wire fences of the camps, or . . . hosed to death with high-pressure water hoses. . . . A prisoner was expected to live on average for [three to] nine months. . . . [The] productivity of each prisoner was calculated to yield 1,631 marks for the Nazi state (the total includes the profit gained from the 'careful utilization of the corpse'). . . . Physicians on duty in the concentration camps . . . killed thousands . . . by injecting poison, or performed . . . painful medical experiments on helpless victims who died miserably as a result."[12]

The rationale for the slaughter of homosexuals is best capsulized by the instigator of gay genocide, Adolf Hitler. Fundamentally, he was awash with free-floating fears and hatreds and saw himself as Wotan the Destroyer, which included his own destruction. ("Hitler's suicide conforms to what is known about suicide in general. In fact, its most unusual characteristic is that it is very nearly that statistical freak, the *typical* suicide," says McRandle.[13] The psychodynamics of creative and destructive components of the psyche, with particular regard to Hitler, are briefly but excellently presented in McRandle's *The Track of the Wolf*.) Hitler rationalized the impending slaughter of gays in this pontification to Rudolf Diels, first Chief of the Gestapo. Diels says of Hitler:

"He lectured me on the role of homosexuality in history and politics. It had destroyed ancient Greece, he said. Once rife, it extended its contagious effects like an ineluctable law of nature to the best and most manly of characters, eliminating from the reproductive process those very men on whose offspring a nation depended. The immediate result of the vice was, however, that unnatural passion swiftly became dominant in public affairs if it were allowed to spread unchecked."[14] Steakley comments: "With its mingled elements of condemnation, dread, and admiration, Hitler's view appears to be a concatenation of eugenics, fear of conspiracy (similar to the 'Elders of Zion' legend), and the theory of homosexual superiority advanced by Hans Blüher."[15]

Beneath Hitler's savagely warped thinking regarding gays lurked something else: a gnawing fear of homosexuality within himself. Everyone is a latent heterosexual or homosexual, as the case may be, and Hitler was no exception. He protested his "brutal" masculinity too much, too often. In Hitler's case—as in Himmler's—the fantasied tough male sex role developed into sadism, murder, and destruction. When he no longer had any further use for gays, their extermination became inevitable because, says Waite, "as long as he prosecuted and attacked homosexuals, he felt he was successfully combating his own inadmissible inclinations toward homosexuality."[16]

For a man who detested the law, Hitler was very legalistically inclined. He wanted the persecution of homosexuals legalized and the law profession obliged by drawing up the infamous Paragraph 175A. Since any major alteration in national German law could not be effectuated without Hitler's consent, we must assume he ordered the law written or at least approved it. Hence, within a year of the Blood Purge the persecution of homosexuals was escalated by the promulgation in June 1935 of Paragraph 175A, the first revision of Paragraph 175 in its sixty-five-year history. Until 1935, the only punishable offense under Paragraph 175 of the German penal code had been sodomy; under Paragraph 175A, nine possible "acts" were punishable, including a kiss, an embrace, even homosexual fantasies. As for the latter, in case you are wondering how fantasies can become detected, the answer is that many gays, like many straights, commit sexual fantasies to paper or in letters, and/or talk about them.

Paragraph 175A broadening Paragraph 175 spurred a tenfold increase in convictions on charges of homosexuality over the number preceding 1933. The law was also used to ensnare whomever the Nazis wanted to get rid of in this particularly vile fashion (aside from bona fide gays), such as dissident clergymen. The law was based on "wholesome popular sentiment" and thus became a handy hatchet wielded by good-thinking common-folk Germans, who denounced gays and suspected gays to the SS, SD, Gestapo, and civil police. In fact, they cried "faggot" about whomever they happened to dislike, regardless of the person's actual sexual orientation.

Under the Nazi concept of the "healthy sensibility of the people," and a theory of justice that condemned certain people to imprisonment and death for their "state-of-being," public convictions for violating Paragraph 175A numbered at least 50,000 during the Nazi regime.[17] (Nearly all of them were later taken out of civil prisons and put into concentration camps, which speeded up the process of extermination.) In 1933 there were 853 convictions, 948 in 1934, about 3,700 in 1935, 5,321 in 1936, 8,721 in 1937, 8,115 in 1938, 7,614 in 1939, 3,773 in 1940, 3,735 in 1941, 2,678 in 1942, 996 in

1943 (first-quarter figure only is available). The figures for 1944 and 1945 are not available.[18] The drop in convictions after 1938 is explained by the fact that the Nazis sent gays immediately to prison or a concentration camp (which, of course, they had been doing all along); but court proceedings after 1938 had become too much of a waste of time and manpower.

The estimate of 50,000 is only the minimum. Not included, of course, are those arrested and interned without trial. The 50,000 figure also does not include all those disposed of in the military, the SA, the SS, and other formations by imprisonment and execution.

A comprehensive report of 175A convictions is difficult because, testifies Franz Neumann in *Behemoth,* "innumerable special courts and tribunals . . . [were] created for specific cases and for specific strata of the population. Each of the four machines, party, army, state, and industry, has an extensive judicial system of its own, with statutes, decrees, courts, executioners, and bailiffs. . . . And above all, there are the people's courts. . . . The defendant has no right to select counsel, produce evidence, appeal, or obtain publicity. There are, finally, special courts called just that (*Sondergerichte*). . . . Here too the rights of the defendant are almost non-existent."[19] Further, Hitler had a court set up especially for him. Neumann says a decree of September 11, 1939, created a "division within the federal supreme court before which the public prosecutor may, on order of the Leader, bring any criminal case he [Hitler] deems sufficiently important to warrant skipping the lower courts." The death penalty was routinely rendered in Hitler's private court. "The first case that came before the special division was one of rape committed by a homosexual, and . . . the demand of the public prosecutor for the death penalty was granted. . . ."[20]

Whether defendants were guilty or not is in a way rather beside the point. The point is that it was not enough for the military to mangle gays, for Hitler and the Party to have gays disappear into "night and fog"; there must occasionally be a public display as an example to other homosexuals. The capital-punishment sentence, says Neumann, no longer had "the function of inflicting a just revenge for a specific crime; it is a deterrent, and the question of its justness in any specific case is no longer of primary importance."[21]

Gays picked up by Party and civil authorities were often

confined under "protective custody," an empty and meaningless "legal" gimmick devised by the Nazis on the pretext that detainment was in the best interests of the person interned. Supposedly, it was for the individual's own good to be held in protective custody in order to shield him against bodily or other harm that might ensue from his having in some way affronted the "healthy sensibility of the people," which additionally ensured the peace and order of the Reich.

Protective custody was enforced retroactively, so that any homosexual who had ever come to the attention of the police prior to the establishment of the Third Reich was subject to immediate internment. In one Berlin district, for example, police had a card index of 30,000 homosexuals. Further, beginning with the *Anschluss* (annexation) of Austria in 1938, homosexuals from Nazi-occupied countries were also interned in German camps. The arrest order was spoken in a cold, flat, bored voice: "Order for Protective Custody. Based on Article I of the decree of the Reich President for the Protection of People and State of 28 February 1933, you are taken into protective custody in the interest of public security and order. Reason: Suspicion of activities inimical toward the State."[22]

Because gays transgressed upon the healthy sensibility of the people (and still do), they were doomed for what they were, not for what they did or might do. Gays stir up a tempest of homophobia because it is not the *act* that so disturbs most homophobes, but the state of being homosexual. To draw an analogy, the anti-Semite is not riled at what a Jew does; he is inflamed because a Jew is a Jew.

Side by side with Reich Minister of the Interior Wilhelm Frick, who demanded that homosexuals "be hunted down mercilessly, for their vice can only lead to the demise of the German people,"[23] was chief drum-beater and anti-gay campaign leader Reichsführer-SS Heinrich Himmler. Himmler saw gays as the scum of the earth, much more so than Jews, and to him it was a moral mission of the highest order to eradicate the perverted vermin. Jews were only swine in his eyes, but homosexuals were the greater malignancy. Himmler did not simply put gays on the extermination list ahead of Jews. He in fact said that he did not want to liquidate Jews.

Himmler once confided to his physiotherapist, Felix Kersten, as recorded in his memoirs: " 'I did not want to exterminate the Jews,

Kersten. I had other ideas on this subject. But that miserable Goebbels did everything he could to make it turn out this way. . . . Up to 1940, the Jews could still leave Germany freely; then Goebbels won out. . . . In the summer of 1940, the Führer ordered that the Jews be exterminated by degrees. He gave this task to the SS and to me. That was the one and only time I contradicted the Führer. . . . I told him, 'The SS is ready to fight and die from myself down to the last man, but don't give us a mission like this.' The Führer became furious and said, 'Himmler, you are being disobedient! What is the meaning of this? This is an order; I take the responsibility for it.' So I had no other recourse. Understand me, Kersten, and I hope that history will understand me also.' " After once witnessing the annihilation process of a trainload of Jews by gassing, he vowed that after the war he would develop a more humane way of killing them. However, he never evinced the same "concern" for homosexuals.

The task of gay persecution and extermination would have fallen to Himmler in any case, but this monster moralist enjoyed his work and tackled it with all the zeal of a wrathful religious fanatic. In a speech he gave on the subject of homosexuality on October 11, 1936, he described the killings of Röhm and other gays during and after the Blood Purge, saying, ". . . we did not hesitate to strike this plague with death, even within our own ranks." He announced plainly and unequivocally his intention to wreak gay genocide: "Just as we today have gone back to the ancient Germanic view on the question of marriage mixing different races, so too in our judgment of homosexuality—a symptom of degeneracy which could destroy our race—we must return to the guiding Nordic principle: extermination of degenerates."[24] Himmler's guiding Nordic principle was a parroting of the view expressed by Professor Karl August Eckhardt, an historian at Berlin University and a member of the SS. Himmler felt that the ancient Germanic modes of executing homosexuals—drowning and burning—"was no punishment, merely the extinction of an abnormal life. It had to be removed just as we pull up stinging nettles, toss them on a heap and burn them."[25]

Kersten once tried to dissuade Himmler from exterminating homosexuals. Kersten asked Himmler why he felt compelled to destroy gays: " 'I can tell you why, Herr Kersten,' " Himmler responded. " 'It's because we mean to get rid of homosexuals root and branch. They're a danger to the national health. Just think how many children will never be born because of this, and how a people can be broken in nerve and spirit when such a plague gets hold of it. If a man has an affair with his pretty secretary, at most she will exert some influence over him, but she won't affect his ability to work. In certain circumstances there will be a child. But when a man in the Security Service, in the SS or in the Government has homosexual tendencies, then he abandons the normal order of things for the perverted world of the homosexuals. Such a man always drags ten others after him, otherwise he can't survive. We can't permit such a danger to the country; the homosexuals must be entirely eliminated. . . . The homosexual is a traitor to his own people and must be rooted out.'

"And if he has children?" I [Kersten] objected. "There are a number of men who have both sexual tendencies, live a normal married life and have quantities of children.

" 'So much the worse,' " was Himmler's answer, " 'for then the homosexual tendency will be inherited.' "[26]

Gays were thus among the first victims to be marked for Nazi genocide, a fact that has gone largely unnoted in history—not because historians dispute it but because most seem not to care. The proof of this is self-evident. Louis L. Snyder says in the preface to his *Encyclopedia of the Third Reich,* "The amount of space devoted to each entry was judged by its relative importance to historians of the era." There is no entry in the book regarding gay genocide. Under an entry titled "Concentration Camps," Snyder says only that homosexuals "were treated in ghastly fashion." Further, he defines Holocaust to mean, exclusively, the extermination of Jews. The truth is that the plight of the gays was exactly that of the Jews.

Homosexuals were remanded as "enemies of the State" to prisons and concentration camps, provided, of course, they did not fall victim to summary executions and fatal beatings and torture beforehand, which were a frequent occurrence. The camps to which Himmler ordered gays to be sent were Level III camps, extermination centers especially established for Jews and gays, although other categories of victims were sent there, too. Actually, there was not much difference in the survival rate between the Level I and II camps on the one hand—work and intermediate-status camps—and Level III camps, with the "exception" of Theresienstadt. It was a beautified show-case camp for examination by visiting Red Cross officials and selected foreigners. It was also a transit station on the way to extermination camps.

Within his own organization, as mentioned, Himmler laid down a simple rule for dealing with gays in the police and SS. They were to receive "special treatment." In a 1937 order that was retroactively applied, he commanded: "After serving the sentence imposed by the court, they [SS and policemen apprehended for homosexuality] will, upon my instructions, be taken to a concentration camp and there shot while attempting to escape."[27] Execution was usually effected within minutes after arrival at a camp. The coyness about ordering that gays be shot while attempting to escape was dropped with Himmler's November 15, 1941, announcement of a decree laying down the death penalty for any member of the SS or the police who engaged in sexual relations with another male. The order was called the Führer's Decree Relating to the Maintenance of Purity in the SS and Police. A circular sent by Himmler to all SS and police units read:

"1. In order to keep the SS and police free from homosexually inclined weaklings, the Führer has ruled that any member of the SS or police who engages in indecent behavior with another man or permits himself to be abused by him for indecent purposes will, regardless of age, be condemned to death and executed. In less grave cases, a term of not less than six years' penal servitude or imprisonment may be imposed. [Himmler never defined what was meant by "less grave cases," but it hardly mattered inasmuch as such cases inexorably led to the grave.]

"2. The Führer's decree will not be published because it might give rise to misinterpretation."

What Himmler meant by that latter instruction is obvious: After the Blood Purge, the Nazis especially wanted to convey an impression that Nazism was a wholly straight Movement. The decree could be publicly interpreted to mean that Nazism was riddled with homosexuals.

Within the SS, commanders were lavish in their interpretation of the decree. SS Central Office Chief Gottlob Berger further ordered that indecency did not apply just to copulation. Lascivious intention to arouse sexual desire would be enough to fulfill the terms of the decree. This included unseemly touching of the body of another male, even when clothed; it also included, according to Bleuel, the act of kissing. Goebbels noted in his diary: "An extremely beneficial decree, and one which will preserve the elite organization from this cancerous disease." Outside the SS and police, among the civilian population, homosexuals and homosexuality were summarily dealt with under the Nazis' Paragraph 175A and Paragraph 1 of the Amendment Law, which prescribed the death penalty. In February 1942 the Reich Ministry of Justice specifically instructed that Paragraph 1 was to apply to homosexuals and those found guilty of committing homosexual acts.

Although Himmler was implacably explicit about homosexual culprits discovered in the SS and police—so much so that he had his nephew, SS Lieutenant Hans Himmler, shot at Dachau for this reason—his and the Nazis' concern with one's state-of-being as much as one's acts once led Himmler into an ambiguous stance toward gays. At one point he thought he might cure homosexuals through a regimen of hard work in a concentration camp plus exposing them to female charms while in the camp. (There was no way to de-Jew a Jew, although a very few Jews were "Aryanized" or otherwise given immunity by influential protectors.) Himmler wondered what would happen if gays could be enticed into having intimate relations with the opposite sex exclusively. Would this then effect their de-homosexualization? Would heterosexual functioning alter their homosexual condition? Would this consequently eliminate the homosexual problem and guarantee the Reich that "the best and most manly of characters" would then become "men on whose offspring a nation depended"?

Himmler thus ordered what one might call the world's first large-scale "anti-H-Persuasion" experiment in sexual reorientation. Attractive young nymphs used in these concentration camp experimental soirées were ordered to try to seduce gays. The latter, naturally, were told nothing about the experiment. If a homosexual refused tender siren offers of sexual intercourse, he was removed from the experiment and from life. The gay who unbuttoned and participated, vigorously and regularly, would later be sent into the arms of handsome young men whose job was to try to trick him into unbuttoning for one or all of them. If he did, that would be the last time he would ever do it. However, if he resisted their steamily tumid invitations and advances, he would be considered "cured" and eligible for release from the camp. Upon release, he would be placed under surveillance by the Gestapo to make certain his gay ways were truly mended. Backsliders were put to death.

Höss mentions the hare-brained experiment in his autobiography: "In 1944 the Reichsführer SS had 'renunciation' tests carried out in Ravensbrück. Homosexuals whose recovery was still in doubt would be unobtrusively set to work in company with whores, and their behavior carefully observed. The whores were ordered to approach the homosexuals inconspicuously and attempt to excite them sexually. Those who were cured at once took advantage of this opportunity, and scarcely required any encouragement. The incurable ones took no notice whatever of these women, and if approached in too obvious a manner would turn away, trembling with disgust. The procedure then was for those who appeared fit for release to be given an opportunity of intercourse with their own sex. Almost all of them spurned the opportunity thus offered and firmly rejected the advances of the real homosexuals. There were borderline cases, individuals who took advantage of both opportunities. Whether these men could be described as bisexual, I do not know.

"I can only add that I found the habits and mentality of the various kinds of homosexuals, and the study of their psyches under prison conditions, extremely instructive."[28]

Some gays got wise to what was going on and had a jolly good time—heterosexually—and thus obtained their release. No doubt these were the "cured" homosexuals Höss was talking about (or straights confined as gay).

Needless to say, Himmler's experiment was not successful. Doubtless, however, it would have been a 100-percent "success" had all gays in the experiment been aware that the choice they faced was between getting it on and going free, or being stubborn about it and thereby consigning oneself to death. Because the results were disappointing, Himmler lost interest in the project and it was dropped. Killing them by maltreatment, overwork, and execution was a simpler, quicker, more direct solution to the homosexual problem.

7

The Camps

Homosexuals consigned to a *Konzentrationslager* (concentration camp; abbreviated KZ by the inmates and KL by the Nazis) were identified by a pink cloth triangle about three-and-one-half inches high (the size varied) sewn to the left breast of the jacket and on the side of the right trouser leg of the prisoner's striped uniform, with the apex of the triangle pointing downward. In many cases, gays were made more instantly distinguishable by having them wear pink patches that were about an inch larger than the classificatory insignia other categories of prisoners were required to wear. Inasmuch as gays were considered the lowest strata of KZ prisoners, and were generally singled out for the "worst" treatment, there were cases in which homosexuals attempted to "upgrade" their status by secretly trading a pink triangle for a Jewish yellow star or some other insignia in the hope of improving the chance of surviving concentration camp internment. This, incidentally, was dramatized in *Bent,* a play that opened on Broadway in 1979. It is about gays in a KZ, among other things.

Interestingly, many reviews of *Bent* were favorable, but a TV critic said on the night of December 2, 1979, that "the play was about two homosexuals who died because they wanted to be themselves"—"gay"—but that this theme had and has "nothing at all to do with the real tragedy of the Holocaust"—that, because of this, "the play's message is so insignificant that it could be delivered on a post card." The critic said he based his judgment of the play partly on information elicited in talks with Jewish friends and relatives who survived the camps. The play's message, aside from the transcendental one of love, can indeed be put on the back of a post card. In fact, it can be done in one sentence: *Homosexuals were primary targets and victims of the Holocaust because of anti-homosexualism just as Jews were primary targets and victims because of anti-Semitism.*

The Nazis wanted gays to be especially visible, more so than Jews and almost all other categories of prisoners. The Nazis' reason for wanting gays to be conspicuous, and the choice of pink, are obvious: The presence of "marked men" in the camp evoked the same reaction as in most prisons: homosexuals were brutally assaulted, sexually abused, and frequently murdered by other inmates, which is what the Nazis desired.

"During the first weeks of my imprisonment," said one homosexual, "I often thought I was the only available target on whom everyone was free to vent his aggressions. Things improved when I was assigned to a labor detail that worked outside the camp at Metz, because everything took place in public view. I was made clerk of the labor detail, which meant that I worked all day and then looked after the records at the guardhouse between midnight and two A.M. Because of this 'overtime,' I was allowed seconds at lunch—if any food was left over. This is the fact to which I probably owe my survival. . . . I saw quite a number of pink triangles. I don't know how they were eventually killed. . . . One day they were just gone."[1]

The homosexual who gave that testimony was very lucky. Normally, gays were denied camp jobs (*Funktionen*) that tended to stave off death. Aside from everything else, guards and vicious inmates made gays the focus of a frenzy of hate and violence that regularly put a more-or-less quick and painful end to their lives simply because they wore the pink triangle. An example is in this account:

"He was a young and healthy [homosexual] man. The first

evening's roll call after he was added to our penal company was his last. When he arrived, he was seized and ridiculed, then beaten and kicked, and finally spat upon. He suffered alone and in silence. Then they put him under a cold shower. It was a frosty winter evening, and he stood outside the barracks all through that long, bitterly cold night. When morning came, his breathing had become an audible rattle. Bronchial pneumonia was later given as the cause of his death. But before it had come to that, he was again beaten and kicked. Then he was tied to a post and placed under an arc lamp until he began to sweat, again put under a cold shower, and so on. He died toward evening."[2] These and similar incidents occurred in the concentration camps at Sachsenhausen, Natzweiler, Fühlsbüttel, Neusustrum, Sonnenburg, Dachau, Lichtenburg, Mauthausen, Neuengamme, Grossrosen, and Buchenwald—which were among camps where homosexuals were interned. There was also a concentration camp in Neuwied intended solely for males under twenty.

Sachsenhausen, located not far north of Berlin near Oranienburg, and Dachau near Munich in the South, and Buchenwald outside Weimar in Central Germany were the first three KZs established in 1933 after Hitler came to power. They were among the most infamous of camps with respect to homosexuals because gays were a principal category of prisoners in those camps. Jews were also thrown into these camps, along with many other assorted categories of persons, but the roundup of Jews took place mostly after the Crystal Night pogrom, November 9, 1938. "Up to then," said Rudolf Höss, who had held command positions first at Dachau and then Sachsenhausen before becoming Commandant of Auschwitz, "Sachsenhausen had been almost free of Jews [Judenrein, Jew-pure], but now came the Jewish invasion" of November 1938. Ernest K. Bramsted says in *Germany* (page 215): "Ten thousand Jews were taken to Buchenwald in 1938, but the great majority were soon released from the camp, provided they were willing and able to emigrate and left most of their property to the Nazis." Presumably, the same situation obtained at Sachsenhausen and other concentration camps.

According to Höss and other sources, the killing of gays preceded Jewish genocide. The Nazi genocide of homosexuals effectively began on June 30, 1934, but the "Final Solution" of the "Jewish problem," though informally conveyed to Himmler in an order from Hitler in 1940, was not officially advanced until January 20, 1942, at a meeting in the Berlin suburb of Grossen-Wannsee, the so-called Wannsee Conference. Within a few months the first gas chamber camps were set up in Poland. In 1938, Himmler, Göring, and Bormann were thinking in terms of a solution that would rid Germany of its Jews by emigration, forced and voluntary, with Madagascar considered as a possible site for a Jewish colony.

On a legalistic level, there is no question that the persecution of gays antedates that of Jews. Germany's penal code Paragraph 175 criminalizing homosexuals and homosexual acts was drawn up in the 1800s. The Nazi extension-revision of Paragraph 175 into 175A, promulgated on June 28, 1935, singled out, as the Nazis prescribed, "sexual vagrants for ruthless persecution." To even touch another man in a suggestive way was grounds for arrest. The new anti-gay Nazi 175A preceded by a few months Hitler's Nuremberg Laws that "outlawed" Jews.

There is a very narrow distance between prejudice and persecution. In the Third Reich, there was no distance at all. Those who were hated were persecuted. Reich Legal Director Hans Frank, himself accused of being a homosexual, made explicit the legal and extra-legal persecution of homosexuals in *Nationalsozialistischer Ehrenschutz* (1938, page 14). He said, "Particular attention should be addressed to homosexuality, which is clearly expressive of a disposition opposed to the normal national community. Homosexual activity means the negation of the community as it must be constituted if the race is not to perish. That is why homosexual behavior, in particular, merits no mercy." If Frank was indeed a homosexual or bisexual, one need not think it peculiar that he would lead the pack in the rooting out and destruction of gays. That type of hypocrisy is not at all unusual.

In addition to routine killings of gays, their destruction was also perpetrated by SS scientists and doctors, although they did not view it as deliberate sadism. The doctors considered their work essential to the war effort. Gays, along with all other categories of prisoners (with certain exceptions), who most closely matched the physical and age profile of the average young German soldier, airman, or sailor were selected for experimentation. One object was to test and perfect medical competency and procedures under simulated field and combat conditions. The experiments nearly always ended in death for the subject because one of the aims of experimentation was to calculate the effects of *in extremis* situations. This is partly why most experiments were conducted without anesthesia. Generally, the doctors did not intend to be cruel; it just turned out that way by "necessity." Gays had their hands, arms, feet, legs, and other portions of their bodies hacked off or blown off or shot off; their eyes blinded; their limbs broken; their bodies burned; and subjected to skin and bone grafts, various medicative measures and surgical operations, etcetera—all done without anesthesia.

The experimentation also served an ancillary purpose among SS physicians, most of whom were *not* mad quacks like the student of philosophy and medical doctor Josef Mengele. They were "ordinary" MDs and scientists doing an "ordinary" work-a-day job. However, the subsidiary purpose of all this horror served Hitler's desire to mold the SS into an exclusive order of steely, merciless elitists. He introduced the idea of *Blutkitt* (blood cement) in training his Elite Guard, the SS. In Hitler's Germany, SS doctors were required to perform or watch medical experiments such as skin grafts and abdominal surgery on the unanesthetized bodies of homosexual, Jewish, Polish, and other prisoners. Other initiates of the SS were forced to kill Jewish babies before the eyes of their mothers. Hitler's theory was that after the SS had participated in such activities they would feel drawn together by the bonds of a common experience. The technique worked rather well.

A gay remanded to a camp under some classification other than as a Pink Triangle stood a slightly better chance of survival, unless, of course, fated for immediate execution or medical experimentation. Among the major civilian categories of inmates other than homosexuals included Gypsies (brown triangle), political undesirables or adversaries (red triangle), Jehovah's Witnesses (purple triangle), anti-socials (black triangle), criminals (green triangle), Jews (two yellow triangles sewn together to form a Star of David), and, before the war, "illegal" emigrants (blue triangle). Jews known to be homosexual had to wear a combination pink triangle and yellow Star of David, with consequences that can be easily imagined. The same applied to all prisoners; that is, an inmate interned under two or more classifications had to wear a combination of emblems identifying him in those prisoner-status categories. It was said that many inmates looked like "rainbows."

An example of how a person could come to be branded with more than one inmate-status-color patch resulted from attempting to emigrate. Gays who tried to flee the specter of the KZ after 1933 placed themselves in extreme jeopardy. They faced winding up as a Blue Triangle or a Pink Triangle or both because would-be emigrants were viewed with suspicion. Quite often, if the Nazis had any doubt about a person possibly being a homosexual, or any doubt about his real or imagined or presumed criminality, including being a "political criminal," the émigré applicant would be turned over to the Gestapo and thence to a concentration camp until a proper investigation and disposition could be made.

In addition, a danger confronting any male desiring to emigrate was that his genitals might be examined to see if he was circumcised—as Jews traditionally are. In later years, woe be to him if he were a Jew, or a gay Jew, trying to pass as "Aryan," or if he could not instantly and concretely prove his "Aryanism." (The Nazis viewed circumcision as a Jewish mutilation of the penis. Even today newborn non-Jewish German males are normally not circumcised; whereas in America circumcision is a standard operation, although its necessity is open to question.)

In every corner of Nazi domination, the circumcision criterion was applied to males of all ages during roundups of Jews for liquidation. A circumcised penis of an infant, boy, young man, or adult could spell death for that person and everyone related to him regardless of whether or not they were in fact Jews. Genital examinations were so widespread that underground surgical operations to restore the penis foreskin became a flourishing, in some cases highly lucrative, and always desperate business, particularly among circumcised non-Jews who did not want to end in a gas chamber or the bottom of a ditch merely for the lack of a foreskin. A more-or-less satisfactory semblance of a foreskin can frequently be effected, depending on the doctor's technique and skill.[3]

With respect to hopeful emigrants, the reason for all the murderous concentration on a skinned penis was that Nazi regulations governing Jewish émigrés grew ever more harsh and financially punitive in the late 1930s until the gate was finally slammed shut. Gentile émigrés, however, were in theory supposed to be dealt with decently. But a male found to be circumcised, who had rightly or wrongly declared he was a "pure-bred Aryan," was subject to immediate arrest because he was suspected of trying to leave the country under false pretenses—i.e., of being a Jew masquerading as a gentile trying to circumvent emigration regulations imposed on Jews. The ever-present danger for gays—Jew or non-Jew—in all this bloody nonsense is that investigation of a circumcised man's case might establish that he was impeccably "Aryan" by Nazi standards but at the same time might possibly reveal his homosexuality.

Émigré applicants who were not homosexually virginal, or who had made the mistake of consorting with gays or had gay friends, very often found their emigration application turned into a one-way ticket to a concentration camp, and that their life expectancy had suddenly become quite short. Once gays were brought, or brought themselves, into view of the authorities, the risk of being found out increased enormously. Considering that there was no right of privacy under the Nazis, that there were Nazi agents and informers everywhere, that the Nazis regimented life on a block-by-block basis, that one's "friend" or neighbor might not be trustworthy or could become an informant on a moment's whim or in a twinkling of spite or could under pressure (or torture) become a betrayer, that the investigative powers of the Nazi authorities were unlimited—then one can fully realize what the SS, SD, Gestapo, and civil police were able to accomplish from January 30, 1933, onward. Moreover, to make their job easier, before 1933 there was a file card or dossier maintained by the police and the German Armed Forces on every homosexual with whom those agencies had ever had any official contact. (Precisely the same information is kept in America today by the civil police, all U.S. government investigative agencies, and the U.S. Armed Forces.)

Along with haplessly circumcised gentiles, suspect émigrés, and actual, potential, or phantasmal enemies, plus a potpourri of other victims, homosexuals were among the first inmates of the first concentration camp, Dachau. SA gays began arriving after the

Blood Purge. The camp was established by Hitler on Göring's command at Dachau near Munich in March 1933, less than two months after Hitler was appointed Chancellor. Before Dachau and for some time afterward, the SA and SS used cellars and hideaways throughout Germany as ad hoc lockups for real or assumed opponents of Nazism. Such places were nothing less than torture chambers where countless doomed prisoners were slowly killed as painfully as possible, or crippled for life, often for no purpose other than to wreak revenge, confirm personal power, or just for sadism's sake. (Brutality in the camps at least ostensibly served the useful [?] function of intimidation, which greatly reduced the need for a large staff of guards.)

In places like the SA Brown House in Munich, or the SS Columbia House in Berlin, the screams of gays and others were so horrendous that pails and blankets placed over the head, and children's music played full blast on a phonograph, were used to help smother daylong and nightlong shrieks of agony. The choice of children's music was a typical Nazi touch. Prosaic neighbors sometimes complained about the "noise," and often moved away to escape it.

All the KZs were modeled on Dachau. The guards were from the beginning SS, although until the Blood Purge the SA appeared to dominate. The principal aims of the camps were threefold: (1) To punish and destroy enemies and undesirables (release was possible, albeit rather rare, for some categories of prisoners, including homosexuals; this is an unavoidable contradiction because Nazi action was not fully consistent); (2) to serve as "hardening" training centers for the SS, i.e., to condition them mentally and emotionally to cruelty and murder in accordance with the express wishes of Hitler; and (3) to form a slave labor pool. While Hitler desired the annihilation of all those whom he chose to regard as undesirables or as enemies, the need for and value of forced labor was recognized. Thus, to some extent in conflict with the policy of extermination, the SS exploited its prisoners by hiring the most able out to armament firms, or using them in special SS industries, and so forth.

The reason for the qualification, "to some extent in conflict with the policy of extermination," is that work itself became a means of extermination, especially in the case of gays. With the exception of those herded directly from boxcar trains, ordered to strip, and then driven into gas chambers, or fire pits where they were burned alive, or quicklime pits where they were boiled alive, or shooting ditches, concentration camp inmates substantially aided the war effort and boosted the national economy significantly. Healthy, young, strong gays and other able-bodied prisoners were routinely selected for liquidation through the simple expedient of giving them food rations below the subsistence level and then by working them to death. "Among the different extermination methods perfected by the Nazi technicians of mass murder, that of immediate death in the gas chambers was by no means the cruelest," says Léon Poliakov in *Harvest of Hate*.[4]

Gays were usually segregated so that the drawn-out process of exterminating them could be made more orderly. This process became known as "Project Pink." A survivor who witnessed a Project Pink action wrote: "The homosexuals were grouped into liquidation detachments and placed under triple camp discipline. That meant less food, more work, stricter supervision. If a prisoner with a pink triangle became sick, it spelled his doom. Admission to the clinic was forbidden."[5] The first authentic account of concentration camp internment of gays regarding Project Pink appeared in a German homophile magazine, *Humanitas,* in 1954. (This nine-year delay from the end of the war is highly significant.) Its author was a physician, L. D. Claassen von Neudegg, who had been imprisoned at Sachsenhausen. These are excerpts from his account:

"After roll call on the evening of June 20, 1942, an order was suddenly given: 'All prisoners with the pink triangle will remain standing at attention!' We stood on the desolate broad square, and from somewhere a warm summer breeze carried the sweet fragrance of resin and wood from the regions of freedom. But we couldn't savor it because our throats were hot and dry from fear. Then the guardhouse door of the command tower opened and an SS officer and some of his lackies strode toward us. Our detail commander barked: 'Three hundred criminal deviants present as ordered!' We were registered, and then it was revealed to us that in accordance with an order from the Reichsführung SS [Himmler], our category was to be put in an intensified penalty company, and we would be transferred as a unit to the Klinker Brickworks the following morning. The Klinker factory! We shuddered, for the human death mill was more than feared. . . .

"Forced to drag along twenty corpses, the rest of us encrusted with blood, we entered the Klinker works. . . .

"We had been here for almost two months, but it seemed like endless years to us. When we were transferred here, we had numbered around 300 men. Whips were used more frequently each morning when we were forced down into the clay pits under the wailing of the camp sirens. 'Only fifty are still alive,' whispered the man next to me. 'Stay in the middle—then you won't get hit so much. . . .'

"[Three homosexuals who had tried to escape] had been brought back. 'Homo' was scrawled scornfully across [a large placard hung around their necks] for their last march through the camp. To increase their thirst, they were forced to eat oversalted food, and then they were placed on the block and whipped. Afterwards, drums were hung around their necks, which they had to beat while shouting, 'Hurrah, we're back!' The three men were then hanged. . . .

"Summer, 1944. One morning there was an eruption of restlessness among the patients of the hospital barracks where I worked. Fear and uncertainty had arisen from rumors about new measures on the part of the SS hospital administration. At the administration's order, the courier of the political division had requisitioned certain medical records, and now he was arriving at the camp for delivery. Fever charts shot up; the sick were seized with a gnawing fear. After a few days the awful mystery of the records was solved. Experiments had been ordered involving living subjects and phosphorus: methods of treating phosphorus burns were to be developed and tested. I must be silent about the effects of this series of experiments, which proceeded with unspeakable pain, fear, blood, and tears, for it is impossible to put the misery into words."[6]

Rudolf Höss wrote:

"In Sachsenhausen the homosexuals, from the very beginning, were kept in a special block. They were also kept away from the other prisoners at work. They were employed in the clay pit of a large brickworks. It was hard work, and each of them had to complete a definite amount of work per day. They were exposed to all kinds of weather, since a stipulated number of truckloads of clay had to be filled daily. The process of baking the clay could not be held up through lack of raw material. For this reason they were forced to work in all weathers, summer and winter.

"The effect of hard work, which was supposed to make them normal again, varied greatly according to the different types of homosexuals.

"It had its most salutary effect on the *Strichjungen*. This was Berlin slang for the male prostitutes who thought to make a comfortable living and shirked any work, however easy. They could not
; true homosexuals—prostitution was just their trade.
this sort were soon brought to their senses by hard
strict discipline of camp life. Most of them worked
great care not to get into trouble, so that they might
soon as possible. They avoided association either
ine or with the viciously depraved type of homosex-
ed thus to show that they really had nothing at all in
homosexuals.
ld be trained in this fashion and then released without
their relapsing into their old ways of life. One lesson
enough, especially since most of them were young
boys.

"A proportion, too, of those who had become homosexual out of inclination, men who through overindulgence had grown weary of women and sought fresh excitements to enliven their parasitical existence, could also be cured of their vice.

"This was not the case with those who had begun by dabbling in homosexuality for such reasons but had later become deeply addicted to their vice. They were comparable to the genuine homosexuals, of whom there were only a few examples. Neither the hardest work nor the strictest supervision was of any help in these cases. Whenever they found an opportunity they would fall into one another's arms. Even when physically in a very bad way, they would continue to indulge in their vice. They were easy enough to pick out. Their soft and girlish affectations and fastidiousness, their sickly sweet manner of speech, and their altogether too affectionate deportment toward their fellows distinguished them from those who had put their vice behind them and wished to be free of it, and whose steps on the road to recovery were visible to any acute observer.

"Those who really wanted to renounce their vice, and were sufficiently strong-minded to do so, were able to stand up to the hardest work, but the others, each according to his constitution, gradually broke down physically. Because they could not or would not give up their vice, they knew that they would never be set free. The effect of this psychological burden on men whose natures were for the most part delicate and sensitive was to accelerate their physical collapse.

"Should one of these lose his 'friend' through sickness, or perhaps death, then the end could be at once foreseen. Many would commit suicide. To such natures, in such circumstances, the 'friend' meant everything. There were many instances of 'friends' committing suicide together."[7]

Höss's remark about homosexuals being kept in a special section away from other prisoners refers to a practice he originated. Here he discusses the reason:

"During the Olympic Games [Berlin, 1936] the beggars and tramps were cleared off the streets and put in workhouses and concentration camps, and at the same time the many prostitutes and homosexuals were rounded up in the towns and at the bathing places. . . . [A three-week moratorium on the anti-Jewish campaign was ordered to avoid an unfavorable impression on foreigners who came to Berlin for the games.]

"The homosexuals in Dachau had already presented a problem, although there were not nearly so many of them there as in Sachsenhausen. The commandant and the commander of the protective custody camp believed that it would be best to distribute them throughout the camp, one or more in each room. I was against this, for I had learned to know them well during my own years in prison. [Höss, along with accomplice Martin Bormann, was arrested and jailed in 1923 for murder. Höss was released in 1928 under a general amnesty.]

"It was not long before a constant stream of reports of homosexual activities began to flow in from every block. Punishment had no effect whatever.

"The epidemic spread. I now proposed that all homosexuals be kept together. They were given a block senior who understood how to deal with them. They were also kept away from the other prisoners at work. They were given the job of pushing the heavy rollers used to level the camp streets. Some prisoners from the other categories, also afflicted with this vice, were sent to join them.

"In this way the epidemic was at once stopped from spreading. Thereafter only isolated cases of this unnatural intercourse occurred, since a strict watch was kept on these men."[8]

Of all camp internees, homosexuals were truly a special category. Generally, not even straight Jews would have anything to do with gays. For the most part, the attitude toward homosexuals among straight inmates combined with that of the guards—to say nothing of Nazi policy regarding gays—helped assure the speedy annihilation of incarcerated homosexuals during the Holocaust.

Raul Hilberg, author of *The Destruction of the European Jews,* who was a member of the President's Commission on the Holocaust, which has been superseded by the U.S. Holocaust Memorial Council, is quoted in an article, "Whose Holocaust?" by Richard Goldstein in the December 10, 1979, issue of the New York *Village Voice* as saying: "Homosexuals had a much better chance of survival in a concentration camp."

Hilberg clarified that statement in a recent letter, saying that he meant that homosexuals had a better chance of survival than Jews. "The formulation," says Hilberg, "covers 1933-1945 and is not a statistical assessment of conditions in a particular camp before or after the outbreak of war." In the *Voice* article Hilberg is reported to have said that homosexuals were highly valued prisoners, and that many kapos—inmates who administered the barracks and dispensed instant discipline (beatings and killings were common)—were gay. The *Voice* says that Hilberg, who is a member of the faculty of the Department of Political Science at the University of Vermont, is opposed to including gays in any memorialization of Holocaust victims. "That would be a travesty," said Hilberg to Goldstein.

In Hilberg's follow-up letter he elaborates: "The unqualified assertion that homosexuals were highly valued prisoners is not an accurate recapitulation of my thinking. Concentration camp inmates were not highly valued by definition. It may be said, however, that even misery is relative. Apart from the question of the position of homosexuals in the hierarchy of the camp population, and without regard to such subsidiary points as homosexuals in work gangs and homosexuals among 'prominents,' it may safely be concluded that homosexuals as a group were better off than the Jews."

Available evidence indicates that gays were *not* highly valued prisoners, and they were *not* as a group better off than the Jews. In overall prisoner ranking, gays were, as a rule, considered the scum of the camp by the SS and most non-Pink Triangle inmates, and were normally excluded from any campling position, such as kapo. However, Hilberg's claim that homosexuals had a much better chance of survival than Jews is doubtless correct in a mathematical sense. For every one homosexual done to death, an enormously greater number of Jews were killed. Also, it goes without saying that in general it was infinitely easier for gays to elude the Nazis outside the camps.

Once inside a KZ, however, gays as a prisoner category were subjected to extraordinary maltreatment. This is difficult to express properly because on the face of it one seems to be saying that gays were treated worse than Jews and other categories of inmates. This is true only in the sense that camp commandants, guards, and kapos made gays a *focus* of barbarity, while Jews and other inmate categories were *routinely* barbarously treated. There is only a slight semantic distinction, in terms of inflicted savagery, between "focus" and "routine." Actually, it is a meaningless distinction in every respect except that of wholly academic historical interest. Aside from certain contrarieties, there was no such thing as "worst" treatment in a KZ.

It may seem insensately eerie to appear to haggle over who was the "doomedest" of the doomed, and I hope I give no such impression here. Yet, some reply must be made to those who say, as Hilberg does in his letter: "I have no precise statistics of practicing homosexuals at the time of the Nazi regime, but it is evident to me that only a relatively small percentage of them could have been arrested, let alone mistreated to death. In no sense may it be claimed, therefore, that they were being 'exterminated,' and any attempt to consider them, along with the Jews, as victims of the Holocaust is, I repeat, a travesty."

One of the most acclaimed and respected authorities on the Holocaust, Eugen Kogon, a political opponent of the Third Reich who was interned in the Buchenwald concentration camp from 1939 to its liberation in April 1945, and who was an expert informant for the War Crimes Commission, says in his book, *The Theory and Practice of Hell* (pages 43-44):

"The fate of the homosexuals in the concentration camps can only be described as ghastly. They were often segregated in special barracks and work details. Such segregation offered ample opportunity to unscrupulous elements in positions of power to engage in extortion and maltreatment. Until the fall of 1938 the homosexuals at Buchenwald were divided up among the barracks occupied by political prisoners, where they led a rather inconspicuous life. In October 1938, they were transferred to the penal company in a body and had to slave in the quarry. This consigned them to the lowest caste in camp during the most difficult years. In shipments to extermination camps, such as Nordhausen, Natzweiler and Gross-Rosen, they furnished the highest proportionate share, for the camp had an understandable tendency to slough off all elements considered least valuable or worthless. If anything could save them at all, it was to enter into sordid relationships within the camp, but this was as likely to endanger their lives as to save them. Theirs was an insoluble predicament and virtually all of them perished."

In response to homosexuals desiring to be remembered as Holocaust victims, Goldstein says in the *Voice* article cited that it "is inevitable that homosexuals would come to 'need' the Holocaust, if only because it simplifies the immensely complicated process by which they come to feel oppressed." This is probably correct—in much the same way it is for Jews or anyone else who was ground to death in the KZs and elsewhere as a consequence of prejudice and mindless oppression. According to the Gay Activists Alliance in Washington, D.C., as reported in the Boston *Gay Community News* on May 24, 1980, the U.S. Holocaust Memorial Council says gays will be specifically mentioned in Holocaust commemorations in America. However, the Alliance noted that "President Carter . . . has ignored requests that he honor the gay victims of the Holocaust."

Surviving the Holocaust, broadly speaking, depended on securing a "cushy" inmate job in camp operations—e.g., a kapo (usually a brutal overseer of inmate activity), cook, carpenter, clerk, typist, orderly, kitchen porter, and so on—all the myriad functions that attended the daily routine of a vast, largely self-contained camp. Many of the jobs were acquired through bribery by those who had access to secreted valuables left behind in the camps by many of those who had been executed. However, straight prisoners and the SS saw to it that homosexuals were with few exceptions excluded from what might have been life-saving jobs. Of course, no job ensured survival, but anything helped. Some *Funktion* was better than nothing because there were few long-time concentration camp inmates who did not in the course of time rise to more favorable, if not comfortable, working conditions. Those who failed in this endeavor simply perished. Gays failed because almost everything and everyone was against them.

Even one last flickering hope was denied them, a remote chance of survival that might have resulted in the saving of the lives of some gays: Near the end of the war there reportedly was a plan suggesting the removal of homosexuals from prisons and concentration camps in order to throw them into the front line to fill out Hitler's ravaged combat units. There is no convincing evidence that the plan was considered seriously at the highest levels, but any thought of implementation was aborted by the disintegration of Germany. There were, however, some condemned gays in the Oskar Dirlewanger Brigade unit, a Waffen-SS penal unit notorious both for its bloodthirstiness and casualty rate. Dirlewanger settled matters of discipline in the unit by taking out his pistol and shooting the offender. This partly accounts for the astounding fierceness of the brigade. The choice was simple for Dirlewanger gays and others: Either fight the enemy without relenting, and perhaps live, or die as the penalty for having failed one's duty. Either obey the most appalling orders to fight or to commit atrocities, or be instantly shot or hanged.

Homosexuals were thus everywhere among two particularly well-differentiated categories of men, according to an Auschwitz survivor—"the saved and the drowned." Gays were disproportionally among the drowned. Primo Levi says in *Survival in Auschwitz*: "In history and in life one sometimes seems to glimpse a ferocious law which states: 'To he that has, will be given; to he that has not, will be taken away.' In the Lager [camp], where man is alone and where the struggle for life is reduced to its primordial mechanism, this unjust law is openly in force, is recognized by all."[9]

Although homosexuals were as a rule excluded from holding any inmate camp position, there were a few exceptions, some blood splattered, the goriest of which occurred at Auschwitz. The SS deliberately sought out a certain homosexual criminal, Ludwig Tiene (which might not be his real name), who had been jailed in a civil prison for sex murders, and gleefully installed him as Camp Senior (a specific position, but also used as a generic term); it was the highest inmate position at Auschwitz. He was interned not as a Pink Triangle but as a homicidal criminal. The beast's appetite was to strangle or crush or gnaw to death good-looking heterosexual or homosexual boys and young men while he orally or anally raped them. That was just his sexual activity. His demonic viciousness was boundless; he capriciously killed inmates, sometimes as many as 100 or more daily. Apparently, it greatly amused the SS to place a homosexual mad-dog killer in a position of dominance over other prisoners.

That was but one example of SS humor. Jews, to cite another example, were regularly appointed as kapos because the SS was bemused by the sight of a Jew beating other Jews with a club, whip, or truncheon. The beatings were frequently fatal. This occurred daily, month in and month out, year after year in all the KZs except Theresienstadt. Poliakov says, "The only possible way of finally adapting oneself to life in this infernal world was by an imperceptible but progressive acceptance of the SS universe and values; . . . imitation of the SS embraced not only their brutality of feeling and cruel behavior, but also such details as vocabulary, general bearing, and dress, choice of amusements, and, insensibly, even the very ideas and sentiments that dominated in the dreadfully mutilated souls of the SS."[10]

According to concentration camp inmate Primo Levi, "They are the typical product of the structure of the German Lager: if one offers a position of privilege to a few individuals in a state of slavery, exacting in exchange the betrayal of a natural solidarity with their comrades, there will certainly be someone who will accept. He will be withdrawn from the common law and will become untouchable; the more power that he is given, the more he will be consequently hateful and hated. When he is given the command of a group of unfortunates, with the right of life or death over them, he will be cruel and tyrannical, because he will understand that if he is not sufficiently so, someone else, judged more suitable, will take over his post. Moreover, his capacity for hatred, unfulfilled in the direction of the oppressors, will double back, beyond all reason, on the oppressed; and he will only be satisfied when he has unloaded onto his underlings the injury received from above."[11]

Becoming a kapo was one of the best ways of surviving a KZ under the Nazis; however, the moment camps were liberated at the close of the war, countless kapos were murdered by other inmates. For gays, sex sometimes helped in the struggle for survival, but its value in this regard was generally ephemeral. As in all prison milieus, comely boys and handsome young men, straight or gay, might be chosen as concubines by kapos, block leaders, and other senior inmates (and often by the SS themselves). These camp functionaries were not necessarily homosexual; indeed, they were usually straight. If the functionaries were gay, they were not interned as Pink Triangles but under some other inmate classification.

As for the SS, their behavior was typical among those who engaged in sexual bestiality. An example is a film, in color with a sound track, that was secretly made for the pornographic enjoyment of a select coterie of Nazis showing a wild drunken orgy of beautiful boys and handsome young men being whipped, raped, and murdered by the SS. Unfortunately, no further details about this film can be divulged. Confidential information regarding it came from a homosexual at the highest levels of the diplomatic service. The film is today very discreetly and very privately shown to only an inner circle of certain homosexuals in Europe, and probably will not be made public in the lifetimes of these gays, for obvious reasons. While this admittedly may seem like fevered fiction, it is nevertheless the truth.

A male concubine was known in KZ argot as a *Piepel* or *Püppel* (little doll) or *Puppenjungen* (doll boy). No choice in the matter was given the individual, though he had the option of being immediately murdered for refusing to become a *Piepel.* On the surface, to be selected as a concubine (and body servant) appeared attractive. The function conferred an abundance of contraband food, liquor, tobacco, and many other normal amenities, the pick of luxurious clothing and furs left behind by those who had been massacred, plus leisure, an uncertain measure of protection from prisoner and guard abuse (but not from abuse by the lover of the *Piepel*). The position also secured chancy exemption from periodic selections for the gas chamber. So long as a *Piepel* remained in favor, his was a seemingly enviable position. "Being Piepel is the highest *Funktion* in the block. . . . And if a Piepel's got a head on his shoulders and not only an ass . . . he can get anything he wants out of his Block Chief."[12]

A *Piepel* did not hold the highest prisoner function in the block, of course, but it certainly was a "comfortable" one, while it lasted, if he could adjust and make the most of it. For a gay, adjustment was fraught with problems; for a straight, adapting could be highly problematical. For example: According to an Auschwitz survivor, Moni, a male concubine in Auschwitz, "so wanted to serve Franzl [Moni's Block Chief] with all his heart. He wants to be devoted to him, shine his boots, serve him his meals, see to it that there are always fresh underwear, clean socks in his locker, the bed neatly made. He so wants Franzl to like him in bed. He is ready to let Franzl try anything he wants on him. At first it had hurt him terribly. Those first nights in the cubicle with Franzl, he hadn't been able to lift a foot afterwards. He had to lie down all day. He lost his appetite and couldn't touch a bite. He had choked down his tears. But after a while he got used to it. Only his appetite never came back. Oh, how he wishes he could give Franzl what he wants in bed. He doesn't let out the slightest groan any more during the lovemaking. Why won't Franzl understand? Why does he kick him out of bed? Moni raised his eyes from the plate and looked around the kitchen. Auschwitz sadness welled in him at the thought that he might lose out on all this."[13]

The above excerpt is from a fictionalized account, but there is not the slightest breath of exaggeration in it. Whether or not the author was a *Piepel* is factually beside the point. He speaks the truth of camp life and death. He was there.

If the *Piepel* kept his good looks, and performed well sexually, he had a better chance of staying alive for a longer period than an ordinary campling who had no *Funktion*. The difficulty in this situation, however, as in all intimate relationships, is that staleness and boredom or just plain fickleness commonly set in. When this occurred, and the concubine was cast away, it usually meant certain death unless he found haven in the bed of another "protector." As often as not, though, his "lover" did not simply reject him but killed him as casually as one swats a fly. Love was not usually part of the liaison. The brutalized and/or criminal elements pervasive among kapos and other camp seniors were steeped in savagery and alcohol. This volatile combination spelled a gruesome finish for many a *Piepel*, a number of whom death caught by surprise:

"They think they've got it made. They would never dream that those boots they polish for all they're worth every morning will suddenly one night go seesawing across their own necks. They can't imagine that the same hands which play with their bodies would ever come to murder them. Try and tell it to a Piepel; he won't believe you. Every Piepel thinks: Maybe other Block Chiefs. But mine? Never! *His* Block Chief is not like the rest. Every Piepel harbors an intimate secret in his heart—the secret of the love which his Block Chief makes to him at night."[14]

In Auschwitz and other camps, says Ka-Tzetnik in *Atrocity*, a *Piepel* was routinely acquired and dispatched thusly: "The Block Chief just waits until he can bring back a new Piepel from the [train disembarkation] platform. That night he takes the old Piepel into the cubicle, lays him on the floor, and puts a cane across his throat. Then he steps on the cane—one boot on each end—and he does a seesaw. And that's all—that is the end of the old Piepel."[15]

The killing was sometimes done with the aid of camplings, who at the bidding of a camp senior would hold down the victim's flailing arms and legs. Accessories to such killings were, usually, pathetically dulled inmates who had almost stopped thinking or feeling. Poliakov says:

"When one tries to define the dominant reaction of the prisoners, it is the general passivity which is most striking. The consequence of this, regardless of what group the prisoner belonged to, was apparently an absolute obedience, a perfect submission to the orders of the SS, their henchmen, block leaders, or Kapos. This obedience actually reached the point of automatism. Even if an order meant grave and sometimes directly fatal consequences for the prisoner, it was nonetheless carried out. This kind of behavior can best be understood with the help of a few examples. The 'beret trick,' an SS amusement in vogue at certain periods, consisted of snatching off a prisoner's cap and throwing it beyond the line of sentries into the zone where they had orders to fire on sight. He was then ordered to go and pick it up; prisoners regularly committed suicide in this way, such cases being listed as 'killed while trying to escape.' There were also the Kapos who would hand a prisoner a rope and order him to hang himself. It was normal at Auschwitz for such an order to be carried out."[16]

Not so resigned to death were gays and others who were delivered "fresh" to the camps for "special treatment." At Auschwitz there was a huge underground room the SS called the Hall of Corpses. It was used for "shambles," as they referred to it in the precise dictionary definition; that is, for shooting newly arrived prisoners who for some administrative reason or other were not processed in the usual manner. For a time, an SS Oberscharführer Walter Quakernack enjoyed the work: Two or three times weekly, says Salmen Lewental in *Amidst a Nightmare of Crime,* "the so-called 'shambles' took place in this hall of corpses; that is, larger or smaller groups, not larger than 250 persons (of different sex and age), were brought here and, after having undressed, were shot. Such persons came from outside the camp, which means they were not Auschwitz prisoners. They had been arrested by the Gestapo in various localities and were brought to the crematorium to be shot without having been entered in the camp records. Auschwitz prisoners were subjected to the 'shambles' in a few cases only. . . .

"I heard with my own ears how they shouted they were not guilty, how the children cried, and Quakernack would reply, 'More of us perish at the front.' Then we were called into the hall where the executions took place and we, Jews, used to take away still warm, bleeding bodies to the cremators. Every hour we would take away 30 corpses. Quakernack stood with the gun in his hand, covered with blood and dripping with it. Besides Quakernack, the Auschwitz Lagerführer [Heinrich] Schwarz and the commandant of the entire camp [Rudolf Höss] with his followers were present at executions of that kind."[17]

Curiously, Höss fails to mention in his autobiography that he was present at shambles' proceedings. Höss's autobiography is otherwise remarkably frank, chillingly objective, as though he were calmly and rationally discussing the killing of cattle in a slaughterhouse rather than the killing of humans in a slaughterhouse. But it seems even mass murderers have a limit to what they will confess. He preferred not to convey an impression in his autobiography that he was a bloody monster; he was "just doing a job." To set an example of cool detachment to his subordinates, he was usually present at all of the various extermination sessions, which, he averred, made him feel "uncomfortable."[18] Höss said in his autobiography (page 202): "Let the public continue to regard me as the bloodthirsty beast, the cruel sadist, and the mass murderer; for the masses could never imagine the commandant of Auschwitz in any other light. They could never understand that he, too, had a heart and that he was not evil."

In Höss's *danse macabre* milieu in the inferno of Death, sex was a luxury. Overall, while there was sexual activity in the camps—female brothels, doll boy brothels, sadistic sex, and so on—sexual expression was generally an indulgence only a well-fed nonterrorized few could afford. Terrence Des Pres reports in *The Survivor,* "The loss of sexual will was a universal phenomenon in the camp world, despite the fact that erotic activity was present in limited degree. . . .[;] sex was possible mainly for special prisoners. Kapos and cooks, for example—men and women safer and better fed—took advantage of their positions and indulged themselves. . . ."[19]

Under conditions of extreme stress, cruelty, starvation, fear, and work schedules and conditions deliberately designed to prove fatal, which applied to most prisoners, the sex urge vanished completely. Inmates report they did not even have erotic dreams. There were many instances of homosexual lovers sustaining each other, providing inexpressibly poignant spiritual comfort and warmth, but sex often was not part of the relationship. Pres comments, "One of the striking things about concentration-camp experience—and there is enormous evidence on this point—is that under conditions of privation and horror the need for sex disappears. It simply is not there, neither in feeling nor in fantasy, neither the desire nor the drive. As one survivor says, 'Many of us young men ceased to have any sexual feelings whatever. . . .' "[20]

Hunger for food entirely replaced sexual hunger—to such a degree that cannibalism was common. One inmate said: "I cannot very well explain my feelings when I first saw one of those pits which already contained many dead and I had to throw my particular corpse on top of those others already there. During the dragging process I noticed on many occasions a strange wound at the back of the thigh of many of these dead. First of all I dismissed it as a gunshot wound at close quarters, but, after seeing a few more, I asked a friend and he told me that many prisoners were cutting chunks out of these bodies to eat. On my very next visit to the mortuary I actually saw a prisoner whip out a knife, cut a portion out of the leg of a dead body, and quickly put it in his mouth, naturally frightened of being seen in the act of doing so. [Had he been seen by a camp senior or guard, he would have been executed—not for cannibalism but for "unauthorized eating."] I leave it to your imagination to realize to what state the prisoners were reduced for men to chance eating these bits of flesh taken out of black [decomposing] corpses."[21] At Auschwitz, Höss tells of finding "bodies of Russians who had been killed by their fellows, partly eaten and then stuffed into a hole in the mud. . . . The mysterious disappearance of many Russians was explained in this way."[22]

The ravages of hunger, for those who could not or would not eat raw human flesh (sometimes camplings roasted it over a tiny fire), usually became terminal after about two months. Poliakov reports that the majority of inmates "quickly traveled the steep road whose inevitable last stage was known in the camp as 'Moslemization.' [They were also known as mussulmen.] This was the term used to describe the state of total debility which preceded death. Most prisoners arrived at this stage of incredible emaciation and utter mental languor after two months in the camp.

"When they could still walk, they moved like automatons; once stopped, they were capable of no further movement. They fell prostrate on the ground; nothing mattered any more to them. Their bodies blocked the passageway. You could step right on them and they wouldn't draw back their arms or legs an inch. No protest, no cry of pain came from their half-open mouths. And yet they were still alive. The Kapos, even the SS men, could beat and push them, but they would not budge; they had become insensible to everything. They were men without thoughts, without reactions, without souls, one might say. Sometimes, under the blows, they would suddenly start moving, like cattle, jostling against each other. Impossible to get them to tell their names, much less the date of their birth. Even gentleness was not enough to make them talk; they would only give you an expressionless stare. And when they tried to answer, their tongues could not touch their dessicated palates to produce sounds. You smelled only a poisonous breath, as though it issued from entrails already in a state of decomposition."[23]

Emaciation and disease as a consequence of starvation led inexorably to the gas chamber, if one did not die along the way first. Periodic *Selektionen* of the unfit kept the gas chambers packed and the crematory facilities blazing. As many as 3,000 people could be gassed at one time in a huge chamber at Auschwitz. The selection procedure within the camps (rather than at train terminals) was simple: Poliakov says, "Cell block by cell block the Germans made the people file stark naked in front of them, and a glance at their buttocks decided their fate, for no part of the human body so faithfully reveals a person's loss of flesh. . . . The skeletons and half-skeletons made an heroic effort for the minute to put on a brave and gay front before the Germans, puffing out their fleshless thoraxes. But the pitiless buttocks allowed no cheating!"[24]

Those most likely to survive a *Selektion,* says Levi, were those with *Funktionen*—"doctors, tailors, shoemakers, musicians, cooks, young attractive homosexuals, friends or compatriots of some authority in the camp; or . . . [the] particularly pitiless, vigorous and inhuman individuals, installed in the posts of Kapos, *Blockältester,* etc.; or finally those who, without fulfilling particular functions, had always succeeded through their astuteness and energy in successfully organizing, gaining in this way, besides material advantages and reputation, the indulgence and esteem of the powerful people in the camp. Whosoever does not know how to become an 'Organisator,' 'Kombinator,' or 'Prominent' (the savage eloquence of these words!) soon becomes a 'mussulman.' "[25]

Of course, there was no defense against starvation, torture, and death in the *Konzentrationslager.* Against a whim or administrative order, there was no protection. Needless to say, shipments of humans destined for immediate execution had no options. One small example of this was a shipment of about 1,000 boys gassed on October 20, 1944, at Auschwitz. In the absence of documentation we do not know how many of these boys were homosexual, only that many of them were incarcerated as such.

A witness to this *Aktion,* Lewental, wrote: The boys "were brought in the middle of a bright day. [They were] aged from 12 to 18, dressed in long striped clothes; . . . their feet were shod in worn out shoes or wooden clogs [prisoner attire]. The boys looked so handsome and were so well-built that even these rags did not mar their beauty. This happened in the latter part of October. They were brought by 25 SS men. . . . When they came to the square the Kommandoführer gave the order for them to undress in the square. The boys noticed the smoke belching from the chimney and at once guessed that they were being led to death. They began running hither and thither in the square in wild terror, tearing their hair, not knowing how to save themselves. Many burst into horrible tears, and there resounded dreadful lamentation. The Kommandoführer and his helper beat the defenceless boys horribly to make them undress. His club broke even owing to that beating. So he brought another and continued the beating over the heads until violence became victorious. The boys undressed, instinctively afraid of death, and barefooted they herded together in order to avoid the blows and did not budge from the spot. One brave boy approached the Kommandoführer standing beside us and begged him to spare his life, promising he would do even the hardest work. [The narrator was an inmate member of a *Sonderkommando* team assigned to cremate the boys after execution.] In reply he hit him several times over the head with the thick club. Many boys, in a wild hurry, ran towards . . . the [other] Sonderkommandos [prisoners detailed to assist in the extermination process], threw their arms around the latter's necks, begging for help. Others scurried naked all over the big square in order to escape from death. The Kommandoführer called the Unterscharführer [SS sergeant] with a rubber truncheon to his assistance. The young, clear, boyish voices resounded louder and louder with every minute, when at last they passed into bitter sobbing. This dreadful lamentation was heard from very far. We stood completely aghast and as if paralysed by this mournful weeping. With a smile of satisfaction, without a trace of compassion, looking like proud victors, the SS men stood and, dealing terrible blows, drove them into the bunker [gas chamber]. The Unterscharführer stood on the steps [leading down into the gas chamber] and should anyone run too slowly to meet death he would deal a murderous blow with the rubber truncheon. Some boys, in spite of everything, still continued to scurry confusedly hither and thither in the square, seeking salvation. The SS men followed them, beat and belaboured them, until they had mastered the situation and at last drove them into the bunker."[26]

During the spring of 1945, when the screams had died away and the blood-soaked earth began to blossom anew with life, homosexuals entered yet another limbo from which the world averted its concern. Homosexuals again became un-persons.

8

Testimony from Berlin

The following testimony by a German of aristocratic heritage, "Herr Wolf" (a pseudonym), now a prominent actor in West Germany, was obtained in a recent interview and is here published for the first time.

* * *

FR: Let us begin with your life as a teenager in 1929. This, so I've heard, is when you lived in Munich and first became aware of your homosexuality.

Wolf: I lived in Munich but I studied music in Milan, Italy. Milan was really my home. I had made the acquaintance there of a young man who became my lover. This was the real beginning of my gay life.

FR: How long did you live in Milan?

Wolf: Three years. Then I went to Magdeburg, Germany, where I was offered a role at the opera house as a performer. I also had a nice friend there. I didn't stay very long in Magdeburg. I moved to Mainz. I had a wonderful adventure with a guy from the ballet company there. I met him again in Berlin in 1930 when I was singing at the Metropol Theater. He worked at a gay bar in Berlin.

FR: What about the atmosphere in small cities like Magdeburg and Mainz? Was it difficult for homosexuals?

Wolf: One had to be very careful in small cities. In larger towns the gay scene was very open—in full flower, you might say.

FR: How did gays get to know each other in those small cities? What about gay bars?

Wolf: I don't know about that. There were no gay meeting places that I knew of in Magdeburg and Mainz. There might have been but I really don't know because I've never been a cruiser. When we gays did meet, at least in my experience, it was by chance or at a party. The thing is that I had to work very hard at the opera, and there was no time left to go to bars.

FR: Did you know about the activities of Magnus Hirschfeld's Scientific Humanitarian Committee and its struggle against prejudice toward gays?

Wolf: It was only when I moved to Berlin that I heard of Hirschfeld and his work.

FR: During the 1920s, Berlin was a center of homosexual life. Did you visit bars there or take part in gay activism?

Wolf: Like I say, the theater consumed nearly all of my time. I never took part in the gay movement, but sometimes we went to gay bars. We usually went to a nice bar called the Silhouette. Everyone went to this place, including all the well-known singers and actors. Ernst Röhm used to go there with his cohort when he was head of the SA. It was at the Silhouette that I met a guy I fell in love with.

FR: What was the biggest change in your life when Hitler came to power?

Wolf: I worked for the famous Rotter brothers, directors of the Metropol Theater. When Hitler came to power they lost their jobs because they were Jews. I was close to them, so I lost my job as well. But I had money of my own and an apartment, so there were no problems. In fact, I had no difficulty getting another job on the stage at another theater. But shortly thereafter the Nazis came for me. One day when I got home my housekeeper said, "A policeman is waiting for you in the livingroom."

FR: Because you are gay, the police came for you?

Wolf: Yes. After the murder of Röhm and the Blood Purge the Nazis began to hunt down all homosexuals. The police raided every gay bar and arrested all homosexuals. I had been denounced to the police by a friend who was tortured into revealing the names and addresses of every gay person he knew. The policeman ordered me to go with him to Gestapo headquarters for interrogation. I was told that it wouldn't be necessary to take anything with me because I would be released in a few hours. I believed him, but it was a lie. It was a typical ploy they used to smooth the arrest process. Those few hours stretched into more than nine months. My lover was arrested, too. I was taken to Gestapo headquarters on Prinz Albrechtstrasse. I was put into solitary confinement in the cellar, and heard screams all the time. Later I was taken up to the third floor and brought before a monster of a commissioner, a Gestapo agent. He at once began to shout obscenities at me and ordered me to stand at attention. When he questioned me I thank God to this day that I was able to keep my wits about me, and pretended not to know the names of any homosexuals. At that time I had no idea who had informed the Gestapo about me.

FR: How long were you questioned? Did they beat you?

Wolf: Others were beaten, but I wasn't. The first interrogation lasted about an hour, and then I was taken back to the cellar. I kept hearing awful screams all the time I was in solitary confinement. There was a light burning at all times in my cell. I didn't have a chair, only a bunk made out of wood without any straw. I wasn't allowed to sit down. They watched me all the time through a peep-hole. If I sat down, someone shouted through the door and told me to stand up and remain standing. There were more interrogations, during which I admitted nothing. Then I was taken to a military prison, the Columbia Damm.

FR: How long were you held at Gestapo headquarters?

Wolf: Four days. Then at the Columbia Damm Prison—I think there were only gays in that prison—I was lucky to have been put in a cell with a very nice guy. We didn't know what they were going to do to us. Not knowing was pure hell. We were always taken back to Gestapo headquarters for interrogation. One day on the way to another interrogation, I found myself seated in a truck next to, I then learned, the young man who had turned me in. He was the son of a well-known industrialist. [The father] knew Hitler personally and had given the Führer great sums of money for his political activities. The industrialist's son told me he turned me in because he had been beaten and was terribly frightened. Odd, but this was a piece of good luck because I decided to tell the Gestapo that I had an affair only with him. By doing this I could keep from mentioning other gays and save them. Thank God I'm a good actor. The Nazis believed me. By the way, I never slept with that guy who turned me in to the Gestapo.

FR: Did you have any contact with other inmates, other than the one in your cell, during your confinement in prison?

Wolf: We could talk occasionally, but not often or for long. I saw many gays I knew. I spent Christmas in a cell with that very nice and attractive guy. I've always been kind of lucky! In the cell next to ours there was a young male prostitute from Steglitz who the SS forced into giving them blow jobs, one after the other.

FR: How do you explain the fact that you were treated relatively mildly? You look like the ideal "Aryan": attractive, tall, lean, blue eyes, and blond. Could this have been the reason for your better treatment?—that you appeared to be the Nazi archetypal Nordic?

Wolf: Maybe, but I think my "better" treatment was due more to my having been a well-known actor. Also, my brother-in-law was very influential and did a lot for me, and even was able to visit me. But the catch was that a Gestapo man was present at all visits.

FR: Did you remain at Columbia Damm Prison for the duration of your confinement?

Wolf: No. We knew we were to be transferred to another prison but we didn't know where. Finally, I was taken to Lichtenburg Prison. This was at one time a castle. There were political prisoners there, but other than them we were all gay. We were taken to that prison in covered trucks. SS guards were present, so we couldn't talk to other inmates. The SS verbally assaulted us during the entire trip. We never responded. Later, we were put into work groups. I often cried. I was afraid. The whole thing was so indefinite as far as time and the outcome were concerned. The food was hideous, but we had to eat it to keep from starving. Each evening there was a game the SS played. There were holes in the walls and they would reach through the holes and play with the genitals of the men sleeping close to the holes. Then they would say they had caught them jacking off, and then they would beat them.

FR: Were there any gay SS guards?

Wolf: No, they were more-or-less straight, I think. They were all rotten people, except for one SS leader. I still remember his name, Brunnhofer. He was a real sweetheart. He came from the area of Bamberg, and was so nice to us. A real angel among devils. Normally, the SS were routinely vicious. One day all the gays who were transvestites were ordered to strip and then were beaten and tortured. This greatly amused the SS. The SS thought it uproariously funny when one of them pushed the head of a transvestite into a toilet bowl and held him down until he drowned. The SS laughed.

FR: Do you think that effeminacy had something to do with the way gays were treated? I mean, weren't queens treated more brutally than those who appeared manly?

Wolf: Yes, of course. That was exactly the case. The ones who were, shall I say, "soft," were the ones who suffered terribly. But they weren't the only ones. I once witnessed the execution of six political prisoners. They broke out but were caught a short time afterward. A heavy table was placed in the prison's courtyard. Every prisoner was forced to watch as an example to us. The political escapees were stripped naked, tied to the table spread-eagle face up, and beaten to death with clubs, one by one. You could see that the SS executioners became sexually stimulated while beating the screaming prisoners to death. It was a mess. There was blood everywhere.

FR: Did anyone ever fight back?

Wolf: Nobody ever fought back. We were much too afraid to fight back. Maybe there was one or two who were stupid enough to talk back, to their painful regret.

FR: Did you have mail privileges?

Wolf: We were not allowed to write nor could we receive any mail. Our parents and relatives didn't know where we were. We didn't know anything. That was psychological torture. We didn't know how long the whole thing was going to last, and we didn't know what they were going to do to us. That was terrible. Not knowing anything.

FR: How did your release come about?

Wolf: I was one of the first gays to be imprisoned in 1934. Heinz Hilpert, one of the most dynamic and greatest men I ever met, who was at that time Director of the Deutsches Theater in Berlin, got me out. He went to Heinrich Himmler and said, "I need Herr Wolf.

He's a good actor. This gay business of his is just an occupational hazard. He's not *really* a homosexual." Hilpert knew I was gay—and it made no difference to him—but, of course, he did not tell that to Himmler. Shortly afterward, Himmler visited the prison and recognized me from my performing days. He walked up to me and started to shake my hand. Then he must have realized that one doesn't shake hands with a prisoner and stuck his hand into his pocket. He asked me how long I had been gay. I lied and said that I had been gay for one-and-a-half years. Then he said, "It's that damned morally corrupt Berlin. I'll take care of that. But you see to it that you get back on the right path!" Then again he made a motion as if he wanted to shake hands with me. And again he stopped himself and quickly put his hand back into his pocket. That was my one and only meeting with Himmler. Soon, the order for my release arrived. Also, I should mention my brother-in-law was helpful on my behalf because he was a very famous stage and screen celebrity, an actor of the first order. He was also the friend of Wilhelm Brückner, Hitler's adjutant. My brother-in-law and Brückner used to play tennis together.

FR: How were you dressed in prison?

Wolf: We had to wear worn-out old police uniforms, with black trousers and blue jackets. Around one leg was stitched a yellow band bearing a big letter "A." The "A" stood for *arschficker,* ass fucker. I guess the pink triangle patch was introduced later.

FR: Tell me about your release.

Wolf: We were put into a truck. The trip lasted eight hours because the SS pigs stopped in a village and got drunk. We arrived late that night in Berlin. We were taken back to that terrible Columbia Damm, where an SA man asked me, "What are you doing here?" I answered, "I'm supposed to be let out." And he told me, "There have been a lot of people who thought that." I can tell you I almost wept, almost broke down when that SA man made that remark. I was put to work in the kitchen. That was supposed to be a privilege. I had to stay in prison for eight more days. During this time a young man was beaten to death by the SS. Rather, I should say he was beaten almost to death and then finished off with a pistol. Nobody told me why. We could hear his screams for two nights. He was gay. When I opened the door of his cell during my rounds of delivering bread, I saw the young man lying there with bloody and swollen genitals, which the SS were flogging. The SA man, whom I spoke with earlier, saw me look into that cell and later commented, "After seeing that you'll never get out of here alive." That night there were a couple of shots fired . . . pistol shots . . . in a Nazi prison you soon got to know the difference in sound between rifle and pistol fire. The next morning I saw a trail of blood leading from that young man's cell to the so-called first-aid room.

FR: How long did you have to stay in the Columbia Damm Prison pending release?

Wolf: Eight days. I was finally summoned to the admitting desk and that SA jackass I had first met told me in a friendly manner to pick up the telephone and call the Deutsches Theater. I did and Hilpert answered. He told me I was to "report for rehearsal immediately." I started to cry. The SA man asked, "Why are you crying? You're getting out." I then was allowed to telephone my sister, who picked me up in her car. When I got to the theater I found out I was assigned a role in a play in which I was a prisoner—a role I had been "playing" the past nine months!

FR: Did you have gay friends who you know were incarcerated in a prison or KZ and never heard from again?

Wolf: Yes. Many.

FR: After your release, what kind of life did you have? Were you afraid of being arrested again?

Wolf: Yes. I was afraid. *Very* afraid. The Nazis ruined what should have been the best years of my life. We gays who were still free were forced to be extremely cautious. We had to be extremely careful because we were frightened of spies and informers. However, I did have some contacts. I lived in Berlin during the entire war. Once the Nazis tried to put me in a "Work Company," but Hilpert again came to my rescue. He put me on the program of his production of *King Lear,* casting me in a role that didn't exist. When I asked him when the rehearsals would start, he told me that he didn't know because he had to write my part first! Imagine that! Rewriting Shakespeare! Hilpert was such an audacious man. I don't know how he got away with it. I guess the Nazis thought he was being creatively innovative. He took parts of other roles and constructed the role of "Bacon," the escort of one of the King's daughters, and so I got a work deferment for "reason of theatrical productions." Theatrical productions were considered essential for wartime morale.

FR: Did certain famous gay actors have anything to fear from the Nazis? Or did the Nazis even know that they were gay?

Wolf: Of course the Nazis knew. They didn't bother non-Jewish superstars, not generally anyway. Many were under the protection of Hermann Göring. The SS knew who was gay and who wasn't. They had a perfect spy system. They knew and noted everything.

FR: Most of the theaters were under Dr. Joseph Goebbels as Minister of Propaganda, but some were under Göring. In which group of theaters—those under Goebbels or those under Göring—was it easier for gays to work?

Wolf: Those under Göring. He didn't show us actors his Nazi character too much. He is the one who said, "I determine who is a Jew and who isn't." Käthe Dorsch, a friend of mine, was always running to Göring's wife in order to save Jewish friends, and Göring saved them every time. Gründgens, the famous actor, let some actors who were married to Jews hide on his farm in Zeesen, and nothing happened to them. Göring knew about this and didn't do anything. On the other hand, Goebbels was a different matter. I once worked at the Nollendorf Theater under a Nazi boss, Harold Paulsen. He was a good actor but had a chickenshit character. He was a *real* Nazi. However, I could work with him fairly well. He knew that I was (1) gay and (2) anti-Nazi, but he never turned me in. Still, it was really dangerous working for Goebbels. He didn't protect his people as Göring did.

FR: What about gay bars? I've heard that, among other reasons, some were not closed down because Göring supposedly kept them open to allow his actors to play around without risking collision with the SS and Gestapo.

Wolf: The only gay bar I knew about at that time was Ellie's Bier Bar, but I was always too afraid to go there. Ellie's Bier Bar was obviously under the protection of Göring. But I was much too afraid to go there.

FR: Tell me something about the day-to-day life before 1933. You were an actor, didn't have any financial problems, and you were living in the greatest metropolis for gays in pre-Hitler Berlin. What was it like back then?

Wolf: Berlin was the most exciting city in the world, much more so than New York then or now. Berlin was at that time really *the* city in the world. Not only with respect to the theater world but also with respect to the gay bars and the whole gay scene. I went to some gay bars before the Nazis came to power. When the Nazis took over, we didn't think it would be as terrible as it actually became. Speaking for myself, I just didn't give politics and the Nazis too much thought. I was completely wrapped up in my career. When the Nazis came to power the bars were still in full swing—but then came the police raids and all gay people were taken away, except for the lucky ones.

FR: After January 30, 1933, when Hitler became Chancellor, did the gay bars mostly close of their own accord or were they shut down as a result of police raids and Nazi persecution?

Wolf: As I've said, the gay bars were all glittery and jam-packed, except for a number that were closed on Hitler's personal order in 1933. But there were some that stayed open until around July-August 1934—that is, until shortly after the Blood Purge. Some of the bars were later reopened as a trap, and, of course, the queens didn't have anything better to do than to go to them. As queens will do, they always had their notebooks with them—with names, addresses, sizes, and how often. This made it an easy game for the police and Gestapo. This kind of homosexual did, I think, the most damage.

FR: Did you read the pre-1933 gay literature?

Wolf: I found Hirschfeld too stupid to be read. Nor did I read the many gay magazines brought out in the 1920s. I concentrated mostly on my career. Occasionally I looked at nude photos in the gay publications. That was a lot of fun. I never got around to reading the more important things.

9

Testimony from Vienna

The following testimony is by Heinz Heger (pseudonym of a ghostwriter), condensed and excerpted from his book, *Die Männer Mit dem Rosa Winkel* (The Men With the Pink Triangle), copyright 1972, and reprinted with the permission of the publisher, Andreas J. Meyer, Merlin Verlag, Hamburg, West Germany.

* * *

My family and I were living in Vienna, Austria, in March 1939 when I was arrested because of being a homosexual. I was 22 and attending college, preparing for a career in teaching. Since I had no particular interest in politics, I didn't belong to any Nazi or other political organization. I had no dislike for the "New" Germany—that is, what little I knew about it. The impression I gained at the time was that Nazis sang and marched around a lot and made noisy speeches. I didn't, yet, know about the underside of Nazism. All the talk at school about the "Master Race" and about Germany being "chosen by destiny" to rule Europe seemed to me silly and foolish.

We were a Catholic family. Very religious. My father, a thoroughly correct gentleman, was a high-level civil administrator who commanded, especially of me and my three sisters, strict respect and obedience. Yet, he was a considerate man even if stern and flinty, and his love for my mother was manifest in every way. He treasured her. She was a good and loving person, a hard person for a woman but always a true friend to me and my sisters.

At about the age of 16 I became aware I was far more attracted to schoolmates of my own sex than to girls. At first, I didn't think there was much of anything odd about it. Then, when my classmates began to develop amorous female relationships and began sex talk the way adolescents do—while I clung to a rapturous infatuation for an upperclassman—I started to wonder about myself.

I enjoyed the company of girls and always felt perfectly at ease with them, but it gradually dawned on me that I was seeing them more as unerotic peers than as objects of sexual desire. I liked girls, but not in a sexual way, though I occasionally attempted to become romantically involved with them. But my heart wasn't in it.

Until the age of 19, I succeeded—so I thought—in concealing my homosexual feelings from my mother, but the burden of not being able to talk with her about my true feelings was too much to bear. One day I told her about myself, about how I really felt.

She said, "It's your life. You must live it as you find it. You cannot be false to yourself. You cannot live in a way that is not right for you. You must accept yourself. There's nothing wrong with finding your happiness in men. But please be cautious about the company you keep. Avoid bad company. Otherwise you might come to a bad end. Try to establish a good relationship. I know about what goes on in the world. A good relationship will keep you out of trouble. I've known for a long time about you. Don't despair. Be happy with yourself."

While in college I got to know a number of guys like myself. We organized a small student body, which became larger when German students flowed in following the Nazi takeover of Austria. By the end of 1938 I found the love I had been seeking for so long. His name was Fred, the son of a Nazi Party boss from Germany and two years older than I. He was sensitive, manly, athletic, and brightly intelligent. He was studying to be a medical doctor. We loved each other so much. We made so many plans. But the Nazis had other plans for me.

One Friday at about 1 o'clock in the afternoon in March 1939 the doorbell rang. I opened the door and there stood a man in a shapeless black hat and black horse-leather greatcoat. He said, "Gestapo," and told me to report for questioning at Gestapo Headquarters in the Hotel Metropol at Morzinplatz at 2 o'clock that same afternoon. He didn't say another word. He turned and went away.

My mother and I were stunned. I grasped at straws, assuming I was being summoned merely for questioning regarding some incident at school. There were some students who were outspokenly anti-Nazi. "It can't be anything serious," I said to my mother, trying to reassure both her and myself. "If it were serious, the Gestapo would have arrested me." Then I looked out the window and saw the Gestapo man at the street corner, watching our door. The thought flashed in my mind that he must have expected me to bolt and run to my lover, or another gay friend, and thus add to his catch.

It was then I knew that something terrible was going to happen to me. I found it suddenly difficult to breathe, and felt very cold, ice cold, in that warm room. My mother must have sensed it. When I left she hugged me and said tenderly, "Be careful, Son. Be careful." She could say no more. She couldn't speak beyond those last few words.

Six years would pass before we would see each other again. Six years. In that time I became a human wreck, and she a broken woman who lived in fear, despairing for my life. She had to endure the contempt of neighbors, for it became known to everyone that I had been arrested because I was a homosexual, and that I had been sent to a concentration camp.

I never saw my father again. Not until my release from a camp in 1945 did I learn from my mother that he constantly appealed for my release to the Reich Ministry of the Interior, to the Provincial Government in Vienna, and to Gestapo Headquarters in Berlin. He was forced to retire in 1940 with only the barest pension. This was because his son had been interned in a concentration camp for being a homosexual. In 1942 he committed suicide. In a note to my mother he begged her forgiveness for leaving her. The last lines of the note were: "I can no longer bear the contempt of the people I know, my colleagues, and our neighbors. It's too much for me. Again, please forgive me. May God protect our son."

When I reported to Gestapo Headquarters at Morzinplatz it was humming with activity. SS men in their tailored black uniforms were coming and going. Other people in various Party uniforms, in civilian clothes, and men in those omnipresent horse-leather trench coats and floppy felt hats, and those wearing gold Party lapel badges were dashing up and down steps, rushing into and out of offices, bustling along the hallways, standing around here and there, laughing, joking, talking, as though this were the best of all worlds. Perhaps it was, for them.

Upon presenting myself, a young SS man—they all seemed so young—about my own age—led me to an area where a sign read, "Department II." We stopped in front of a door and an SS clerk announced me and showed me in.

The SS man clicked his heels with an explosive crack, jutted out his hand in the Nazi salute, and then disappeared. The man I now faced was seated behind an enormous desk. I remember he wore a dark suit, with a gold Party badge in his lapel. He was writing with a scratchy pen. His hair was cut in the style of a brush-cut, or crew-cut, very severe. It was as if most of his head had been skinned and the remaining hair stood straight up on end. His desk was piled high with neat stacks of file folders. He did not look up, but kept on writing in silence.

I stood and waited. After several minutes, still nothing. It was very quiet. I could hear a clock ticking. I began to perspire heavily. The man behind the desk kept on writing. Still nothing but the busy scratching of his pen. Then suddenly he stopped. He looked at me with blank, stone-gray eyes. "You're a queer, a homosexual. Yes?"

It was like being hit in the face. "No, no, that's not true," I stuttered. My mouth was cotton dry.

"Don't lie to me, you goddamn cocksucker!" he shouted. "I've got proof."

He threw a photograph across the desk. It was a snapshot of Fred and me with our arms draped around each other's shoulders.

"That's a friend from school, Fred," I said as casually as I could manage.

"Don't give me that shit. You queer pigs have been screwing each other! Do you deny it?" The Gestapo man's lips were a thin, sour red line.

I shook my head. I couldn't speak. A darkness descended. Everything was coming apart. My world was coming apart. I began to tremble.

The Gestapo man leaned forward. With a perfectly manicured forefinger nail he flipped over the photo. I knew what would be written on the back of it, and my heart seemed to stop. "To My Friend With Eternal Love and Deepest Affection" was written on the back of the photo. I had given it to Fred in 1938. My first thought was that it must have been stolen. How else could the Gestapo get the photo? Did Fred . . . was Fred . . . ?

"Is that your handwriting and signature?"

"Yes."

"Good. Sign this."

He shoved a printed form in front of me. I signed, my hand trembling. Everything was blurry. Then I realized tears were streaming down my face. The Gestapo agent pressed a button on his desk. An SS man appeared in the doorway.

"Take him away."

He opened another file on his desk and did not look at me again.

I was taken to a police station where I asked to phone my mother. I was told not to bother because I would "never see home again."

I was put into a cell with two other men. Both were criminals. They immediately began to badger me about the reason for my imprisonment. I told them I did not know. I learned they were both married and in their early 30s.

They found out from a leering guard that I was a homosexual, and immediately began propositioning me. I rejected their advances. This made them furious and they began to condemn me and "all fucking faggots," who, they said, should be exterminated. That night I saw them making it together, and they didn't care that I saw everything. In their logic it was just a temporary digression. They were no doubt right, but it seemed split-brained to me—to spit on gays while enjoying themselves homosexually.

I was brought to trial two weeks later and sentenced by an Austrian court to six months' hard labor for having "willfully engaged in homosexual activity with another person." The proceedings against Fred were dropped on the grounds of "mental confusion." Fred's father, a high-ranking Party official, had probably influenced the court's decision. I never learned what happened because I never saw Fred again. His father had, I assume, found that photo of Fred and me and turned me in to the Gestapo. Doubtless he wanted to break up our relationship and scare Fred into going sexually straight. In spite of all my inquiries and searching after 1945, I never found out what became of Fred. I did, however, learn that his father had shot himself in 1945 when Germany lost the war.

When my sentence was up I was informed I had been reclassified by the Central Bureau of State Security as a prisoner detainee, and was to be held in "protective custody." I was told I was to be sent to a concentration camp. I was shattered. While in prison I learned that "queers" had little chance of survival in a concentration camp.

One night about forty of us were herded into a prison van and deposited at the Vienna freightyard terminal, where a train stood waiting for us. The train was made up of cattle cars and freight cars with window slots that were heavily wired. The trip took us through Salzburg, Munich, Frankfurt, Leipzig, and, finally, Berlin-Oranienburg. The trip took thirteen days. Every evening we were taken from the train to a local prison to spend the night. Sometimes we were hauled away in trucks, but usually the journey was on foot. When taken on foot we would be chained together. It was strange how our chains banged and rattled like some slave caravan out of the Middle Ages. People along the way stared at us with alarm, some with sympathy or curiosity, but most looked at us with complete, blank indifference.

Two inmates next to me in the train turned out to be killers who had been sentenced to death. They showed no remorse over what they had done, and actually took a kind of professional pride in describing their crimes. They extracted from me that I was a "fucking queer," which is what they constantly called me. They forced me to suck them off, ramming their organs alternately into my mouth while I kneeled in front of them. They did this in unison several times each day and night during the train journey.

At the end of the trip was the Sachsenhausen concentration camp. In Sachsenhausen we gays had to wear pink triangular patches that were three-quarters of an inch to one inch larger than all the different patches other classifications of prisoners wore so that anyone could easily spot who the homosexuals were. It was the Jews, the homosexuals, and the Gypsies who seemed to suffer most, who were beaten the most. Singled out as the scum of the earth, we were told we had no right to tread on German soil and would therefore be exterminated. I heard these words repeated constantly by the camp commander and his SS staff and guards. The worst scum of all were those men wearing the pink triangle, so we were told.

We were herded onto the assembly field, and a number of young SS Squad Leaders rushed at us and began beating us with whips and truncheons. We were made to assemble in a five-row formation. Then our names were read aloud from a roster, whereupon each prisoner had to step forward and repeat his name and state his crime. When my name was called out, I stepped forward and stated my name and "crime."

"Okay, faggot, get your ass over there, you cocksucker," was the response. I was slugged from behind and shoved in front of the SS Senior Squad Leader who had my barracks block under his command. As soon as I came within his reach he struck me twice across my face with a truncheon. I fell to the ground. Then I was forced to rise and stand in front of him at attention. Suddenly, he rammed his knee into my genitals, causing me to collapse in agony. A prisoner nearby whispered, "Get up before he beats you to death." When I stood and faced the SS Block Leader again, he smiled at me and said, "That was just to show you, you fucking queer, who your Block Leader is."

The Block Leader and a few SS guards double-timed us to our block, commanding along the way: "Hit the ground, get up, hit the ground, get up," until, arriving in front of our hut block, we were made to line up in a three-row formation. Next, we had to undress completely and place our clothing, with our shoes on top, on the ground in front of us, and wait.

The temperature was below freezing and an icy wind swept down the camp road, but now here we were being forced to stand naked and barefoot in the snow and . . . wait. An SS Squad Leader wearing a leather winter coat with fur-collar trim walked through the ranks striking this or that prisoner with a whip. He would shout over and over, "You pack of queers! You goddamn fairies!" When he passed, he would step on a prisoner's toes with his heavy boots, causing the victim to cry out in pain. When a prisoner moaned the SS Leader would jab the butt-end of his whip into the man's stomach.

I lost track of how long we stood at attention in the snow, but finally we were allowed inside the hut, still naked and barefoot. Next, we were issued regulation prison outfits. Each prisoner was tossed a set of KZ [concentration camp] clothes and shoes without any respect to size. The pants I received were too short and came down to just below my knees. My jacket shirt was too tight, with sleeves that were too short. The coat fitted reasonably well. The shoes were too big and stank with sweat, but had leather soles. This made walking easier than it did for many other newcomers who were given shoes with wooden soles.

We were ordered to fall out in front of our block to receive a briefing by the camp leader. Our block was occupied exclusively by homosexuals, each wing containing approximately 250 men. At night, we were ordered to sleep only in our jackets, with our hands on top of the blankets. "We don't want you fucking faggots to jack off!"

The windows were covered with a thick crust of snow and ice. Anyone caught in bed with his hands under the blanket was drenched with pails of ice-cold water, then made to stand outdoors for an hour or more. Few prisoners survived this treatment. Any Pink Triangle who became sick was handed over to SS doctors and rarely came back alive. Prisoners wearing pink triangles were especially sought for medical experiments. These experiments were always torture—and nearly always fatal.

Our block kapos were Green Triangles—criminals. They were pitiless and extremely cruel. We feared them as much as the SS.

No homosexual was permitted to hold any campling position, or have any authority, with but few exceptions. I was fortunate. I became one of the exceptions. Generally, we homosexuals were not allowed to communicate with prisoners wearing different-colored patches. This was to prevent "enticing" other prisoners into homosexual activity. That was ironical. In other blocks where inmates were treated a little better and where not a single prisoner wore a pink patch, homosexual activity was far more widespread than it was among us "queers."

We were forbidden to approach the other blocks within five-and-a-half yards. Violators received fifteen to twenty strokes of a club or whip on the buttocks. Prisoners wearing other-colored patches were not allowed to enter our compound. We were totally isolated—consigned and doomed to the lowest among the damned, the so-called cesspool of the concentration camp. We were marked for extermination. We were subjected to every form of torture inflicted by the SS and kapos.

The daily routine began at 6 A.M., in summertime at 5 A.M. Breakfast consisted of watered-down gruel and a small piece of bread. Lining up in eight-row formations, we were then marched off to roll call. Afterward, we were assigned work that lasted, in the winter, from 7:30 A.M. to 8 P.M. After work, we returned to the block huts for evening roll call. At roll calls, everyone had to be present, including inmates who had died or been killed at work or during the night. They would be dragged by us into the ranks and included in the count. After roll call the corpses would be taken to the crematorium and thrown into a room to await cremation.

Disabled prisoners also, of course, had to report for rollcall. Countless times we supported or dragged along a fellow inmate who had been beaten by the SS or a kapo, or who was half-frozen or ill. One absentee in the block brought down a hail of savage beatings.

When we weren't doing useful work we had to do "crazy" work designed to be deliberately idiotic and back-breaking, and calculated to extinguish both dignity and life. Pink Triangles were invariably given such work. What we had to do was, each morning, take snow that was in front of our block and carry it from one side of the road to the other side. In the afternoon, we had to take it all back again. To perform the work, we were required to put our jackets on backward and haul away the snow in a lap-fold created by holding up the right and left edges of the back of the jacket. The snow had to be shoveled up by the handful, with bare hands. We had no gloves. We were commanded to work at this task at breakneck speed all day long. That form of physical and psychological torture lasted six days, until a new batch of prisoners wearing pink triangles was delivered to our block and relieved us. In the summertime, the same work routine would be done by all incoming prisoners, hauling sand.

Life became a mocking and cruel and hideous burden. Only in death was there peace. I survived six years' internment in concentration camps, but, in a concrete sense, my life really ended that Friday afternoon in March 1939 at Gestapo Headquarters in the Hotel Metropol at Morzinplatz in Vienna, Austria—the eternal and beautiful city of light, of love, of laughter, of gaiety, of lilting Strauss waltzes.

Notes

1. Welcome to Germany

1. Robert G. L. Waite, *The Psychopathic God: Adolf Hitler,* p. 42.
2. T. L. Jarman, *The Rise and Fall of Nazi Germany,* p. 128.
3. Jeremy Noakes and Geoffrey Pridham, eds., *Documents on Nazism 1919-1945,* p. 36.
4. Richard Hanser, *Putsch! How Hitler Made Revolution,* p. 232.
5. Waite, op. cit., pp. 54, 237-38.
6. Richard Grunberger, *The 12-Year Reich: A Social History of Nazi Germany 1933-1945,* p. 15.
7. Friedrich Meinecke, *The German Catastrophe: Reflections and Recollections,* p. 32.
8. Waite, op. cit., p. 233.
9. Hanser, op. cit., pp. 232-33.
10. Michael Davidson, *The World, the Flesh and Myself,* p. 151.
11. Ibid., p. 150.
12. Ibid., p. 152.
13. Hanser, op. cit., p. 235.
14. Davidson, op. cit., p. 154.
15. Loc. cit.
16. William Sheridan Allen, ed., *The Infancy of Nazism: The Memoirs of Ex-Gauleiter Albert Krebs, 1923-1933,* p. 184.
17. See Konrad Heiden, *Hitler: A Biography,* p. 345.
18. Gottfried Feder, *Hitler's Official Programme and Its Fundamental Ideas,* passim.

19. Davidson, op. cit., p. 152.
20. H. R. Knickerbocker, *Is Tomorrow Hitler's?: 200 Questions on the Battle of Mankind,* p. 3.

2. *The Nazi Aurora*

1. Hanser, op. cit., p. 249.
2. Hans Peter Bleuel, *Sex and Society in Nazi Germany,* p. 30.
3. Robert G. L. Waite, ed., *Hitler and Nazi Germany,* p. 4.
4. Waite, *Psychopathic God,* p. 342.
5. Frederick B. Artz, *1917 and 1941,* p. 16.
6. Knickerbocker, op. cit., pp. 50-51.
7. Hanser, op. cit., pp. 238-39.
8. Waite, *Hitler and Nazi Germany,* p. 17.
9. Knickerbocker, op. cit., p. 2.
10. Waite, *Psychopathic God,* p. 378.
11. Knickerbocker, op. cit., p. 14.
12. Waite, *Psychopathic God,* p. 81.
13. A. J. Ryder, *Twentieth-Century Germany: From Bismarck to Brandt,* pp. 367-68.
14. Waite, *Psychopathic God,* p. 383.

3. *Dragons' Teeth*

1. Hendrik de Leeuw, *Sinful Cities of the Western World,* p. 223.
2. See H. W. Koch, *The Hitler Youth: Origins and Development 1922-45,* pp. 24-25.
3. Waite, *Psychopathic God,* p. 300.
4. James H. McRandle, *The Track of the Wolf,* p. 54.
5. Waite, *Psychopathic God,* p. 301.
6. Koch, op. cit., p. 29.
7. Loc. cit.
8. Koch, op. cit., p. 27.
9. Loc. cit.
10. James D. Steakley, *The Homosexual Emancipation Movement in Germany,* pp. 55-56.
11. Ibid., p. 56.
12. Bleuel, op. cit., p. 245.
13. J. G. Siebert, *The Re-Making of German Youth,* p. 20.

4. *Juggernaut*

1. E. Y. Hartshorne, *German Youth and the Nazi Dream of Victory,* p. 12.
2. Allen, op. cit., p. 242.

3. Ryder, op. cit., p. 236.
4. Waite, *Psychopathic God,* p. 335.
5. Grunberger, op. cit., p. 267.
6. Allen, op. cit., p. 242.
7. William Sheridan Allen, *The Nazi Seizure of Power: The Experience of a Single German Town 1930-1935,* p. 25.
8. Allen, *Infancy of Nazism,* p. 271.

5. Blood Purge

1. Robert Goldston, *The Life and Death of Nazi Germany,* p. 73.
2. Knickerbocker, op. cit., pp. 34-35.
3. Samuel Igra, *Germany's National Vice,* p. 67.
4. Roger Manvell and Heinrich Fraenkel, *The Canaris Conspiracy: The Secret Resistance to Hitler in the German Army,* pp. 12-13.
5. Peter Hoffmann, *The History of the German Resistance 1933-1945,* p. 39.
6. Loc. cit.
7. Heiden, op. cit., p. 381.
8. Bleuel, op. cit., p. 222.
9. Grunberger, op. cit., p. 384.
10. Ibid., pp. 348-49.
11. Bleuel, op. cit., p. 4.
12. Heiden, op. cit., pp. 219-20.
13. Ibid., p. 400.
14. Allen, *Infancy of Nazism,* p. 274.
15. Ibid., p. 275.
16. Ryder, op. cit., pp. 309-10.
17. Jarman, op. cit., p. 156.
18. Allen, *Infancy of Nazism,* p. 315.
19. Hermann Glaser, *The Cultural Roots of National Socialism,* p. 40.
20. Helmut Krausnick et al., *Anatomy of the SS State,* p. 408.
21. Hermann Rauschning, *The Voice of Destruction,* p. 92.
22. Ibid., pp. 93-94.
23. Ryder, op. cit., p. 311.
24. Jarman, op. cit., p. 159.
25. Ibid., p. 161.
26. Ibid., pp. 158-59.
27. Heiden, op. cit., p. 219.
28. Ibid., pp. 215-16.
29. Bleuel, op. cit., pp. 97-98.
30. Ibid., p. 97.
31. Helmut Klotz, *The Berlin Diaries: May 30, 1932-January 30, 1933,* p. 131.
32. Bleuel, op. cit., p. 99.
33. Ibid., p. 100.

34. Ibid., p. 99.
35. Ibid., p. 100.
36. Louis L. Snyder, *Encyclopedia of the Third Reich,* p. 141.
37. Loc. cit.
38. Norman H. Baynes, ed., *The Speeches of Adolf Hitler: April 1922-August 1939,* Vol. I, p. 289.
39. John W. Wheeler-Bennett, *The Nemesis of Power: The German Army in Politics 1918-1945,* p. 320.
40. Joseph Goebbels, *Final Entries 1945: The Diaries of Joseph Goebbels,* p. 305.
41. Grunberger, op. cit., p. 122.
42. Harold D. Lasswell and Daniel Lerner, eds., *World Revolutionary Elites: Studies in Coercive Ideological Movements,* p. 276.
43. Wheeler-Bennett, op. cit., p. 310.
44. Constantine Fitzgibbon, *Denazification,* p. 44.
45. Knickerbocker, op. cit., p. 39.
46. Bleuel, op. cit., p. 101.
47. Loc. cit.
48. David Irving, *The War Path: Hitler's Germany, 1933-1939,* p. 38.
49. Konrad Heiden, *Der Fuehrer: Hitler's Rise to Power,* p. 763.
50. Bleuel, op. cit., pp. 218-19.
51. Heiden, *Der Fuehrer,* p. 763.
52. Grunberger, op. cit., p. 63.

6. Gay Genocide

1. World Committee for the Victims of Fascism, *Brown Book of the Hitler Terror,* pp. 158-61.
2. Steakley, op. cit., p. 105.
3. Ibid., p. 84.
4. Stefan Lorant, *I Was Hitler's Prisoner: A Diary,* p. 8.
5. Ibid., pp. 101-02.
6. Steakley, op. cit., pp. 106-08.
7. Wellington Long, *The New Nazis of Germany,* p. 137.
8. Rudolf Höss, *Commandant of Auschwitz: The Autobiography of Rudolf Höss,* p. 217.
9. James K. Pollock and Harlow J. Heneman, eds., *The Hitler Decrees,* p. 10.
10. Ibid., p. 77.
11. Felix Kersten, *The Kersten Memoirs: 1940-1945,* p. 59.
12. Waite, *Hitler and Nazi Germany,* pp. 70-71.
13. McRandle, op. cit., pp. 150-51.
14. Steakley, op. cit., pp. 109-10.
15. Ibid., p. 110.
16. Waite, *Psychopathic God,* pp. 236-37.
17. Steakley, op. cit., pp. 110-11.

18. Ibid., p. 111.
19. Franz Neumann, *Behemoth: The Structure and Practice of National Socialism 1933-1944*, pp. 455-56.
20. Ibid., p. 456.
21. Ibid., p. 457.
22. Jarman, op. cit., p. 180.
23. Steakley, op. cit., p. 118.
24. Harry Schulze-Wilde, *Das Schicksal der Verfemten: Die Verfolgung der Homosexuellen im Dritten Reich und Ihre Stellung in der Heutigen Gesellschaft*, p. 36.
25. Steakley, loc. cit.
26. Kersten, op. cit., pp. 57-58.
27. Steakley, op. cit., p. 112.
28. Höss, op. cit., p. 105.

7. *The Camps*

1. Wolfgang Harthauser, *Das Grosse Tabu: Zeugnisse und Dokumente zum Problem der Homosexualität*, pp. 30-31.
2. Ibid., p. 32.
3. Jacob Glatstein et al., eds., *Anthology of Holocaust Literature*, pp. 393-94.
4. Léon Poliakov, *Harvest of Hate: The Nazi Program for the Destruction of the Jews of Europe*, p. 223.
5. Harthauser, op. cit., p. 32.
6. Steakley, op. cit., pp. 114-15.
7. Höss, op. cit., pp. 103-05.
8. Ibid., p. 101.
9. Primo Levi, *Survival in Auschwitz: The Nazi Assault on Humanity*, p. 80.
10. Poliakov, op. cit., p. 222.
11. Levi, op. cit., pp. 82-83.
12. Ka-Tzetnik 135633 (pseudonym for Yehiel De-Nur), *Atrocity*, p. 18. Ka-Tzetnik is the German phonetic pronunciation of KZ—inmate abbreviation for "concentration camp"—and 135633 was De-Nur's KZ inmate serial number, which was tattooed on his arm, as was done to all inmates who received a number. The majority of people sent to concentration camps after May 1941 did not receive a number because they were immediately killed upon arrival.
13. Ibid., p. 39.
14. Ibid., p. 86.
15. Ibid., p. 22.
16. Poliakov, op. cit., pp. 220-21.
17. Salmen Lewental et al., *Amidst a Nightmare of Crime: Manuscripts of Members of Sonderkommando*, pp. 40-44.
18. Höss, op. cit., p. 24.

19. Terrence Des Pres, *The Survivor: An Anatomy of Life in the Death Camps*, p. 190.
20. Ibid., p. 189.
21. Gerald Reitlinger, *The Final Solution: The Attempt to Exterminate the Jews of Europe 1939-1945*, p. 469.
22. Höss, op. cit., p. 136.
23. Poliakov, op. cit., pp. 222-23.
24. Ibid., p. 207.
25. Levi, op. cit., p. 81.
26. Lewental, op. cit., pp. 177-78.

Bibliography

Allen, William Sheridan, ed. *The Infancy of Nazism: The Memoirs of Ex-Gauleiter Albert Krebs 1923-1933.* New Viewpoints, New York; 1976.

______. *The Nazi Seizure of Power: The Experience of a Single German Town 1930-1935.* Quadrangle Books, Chicago; 1965.

Artz, Frederick B. *1917 and 1941.* Farrar & Rinehart, Inc., New York; 1941.

Baynes, Norman H., ed. *The Speeches of Adolf Hitler: April 1922-August 1939,* Vol. I. Howard Fertig, Inc., New York; 1969.

Bleuel, Hans Peter. *Sex and Society in Nazi Germany.* J. B. Lippincott Co., New York; 1973.

Bullough, Vern L. *Homosexuality: A History.* New American Library, New York; 1979.

Cohen, Elie A. *Human Behavior in the Concentration Camp.* W. W. Norton & Co., Inc., New York; 1953.

Davidson, Michael. *The World, the Flesh and Myself.* Arthur Barker Ltd., London; 1962.

Feder, Gottfried. *Hitler's Official Programme and Its Fundamental Ideas.* Howard Fertig, Inc., New York; 1971.

Fest, Joachim C. *Hitler.* Harcourt Brace Jovanovich, Inc., New York; 1974.

Fitzgibbon, Constantine. *Denazification.* Michael Joseph Ltd., London; 1969.

Gisevius, Hans Bernd. *To the Bitter End.* Houghton Mifflin Co., Boston; 1947.

Glaser, Hermann. *The Cultural Roots of National Socialism.* University of Texas Press, Austin; 1978.

Glatstein, Jacob, et al., eds. *Anthology of Holocaust Literature.* The Jewish Publication Society of America, Philadelphia; 1969.

Goebbels, Joseph. *Final Entries 1945: The Diaries of Joseph Goebbels.* Avon, New York; 1979.

Goldston, Robert. *The Life and Death of Nazi Germany.* The Bobbs-Merrill Co., Inc., Indianapolis; 1967.

Grunberger, Richard. *The 12-Year Reich: A Social History of Nazi Germany 1933-1945.* Holt, Rinehart and Winston, New York; 1971.

Hanser, Richard. *Putsch! How Hitler Made Revolution.* Peter H. Wyden, Inc., New York; 1970.

Harthauser, Wolfgang. *Das Grosse Tabu: Zeugnisse und Dokumente zum Problem der Homosexualität.* Rütten & Loening, Munich, Germany; 1967.

Hartshorne, E. Y. *German Youth and the Nazi Dream of Victory.* Farrar & Rinehart, Inc., New York; 1941.

Heger, Heinz. *Die Männer Mit dem Rosa Winkel.* Merlin Verlag, Hamburg, Germany; 1972.

Heiden, Konrad. *Der Fuehrer: Hitler's Rise to Power.* Howard Fertig, Inc., New York, 1968.

———. *Hitler: A Biography.* AMS Press, New York; 1975.

Höss, Rudolf. *Commandant of Auschwitz: The Autobiography of Rudolf Höss.* The World Publishing Co., Cleveland; 1959.

Hoffmann, Peter. *The History of the German Resistance 1933-1945.* The MIT Press, Cambridge, Mass.; 1977.

Igra, Samuel. *Germany's National Vice.* Quality Press Ltd., London; 1945.

Irving, David. *The War Path: Hitler's Germany, 1933-1939.* The Viking Press, New York; 1978.

Jarman, T. L. *The Rise and Fall of Nazi Germany.* New York University Press, New York; 1964.

Ka-Tzetnik 135633 [pseudonym for Yehiel De-Nur]. *Atrocity.* Lyle Stuart, Inc., New York; 1963.

Kersten, Felix. *The Kersten Memoirs: 1940-1945.* The Macmillan Co., New York; 1957.

Klotz, Helmut. *The Berlin Diaries: May 30, 1932-January 30, 1933.* William Morrow & Co., New York; 1934.

Knickerbocker, H. R. *Is Tomorrow Hitler's?: 200 Questions on the Battle of Mankind.* Reynal & Hitchcock, New York; 1941.

Koch, H. W. *The Hitler Youth: Origins and Development 1922-45.* Stein and Day, Briarcliff Manor, N.Y.; 1976.

Kogon, Eugen. *The Theory and Practice of Hell.* Octagon Books, New York; 1976.

Krausnick, Helmut, et al. *Anatomy of the SS State.* Walker and Co., New York; 1968.

Kuper, Jack. *Child of the Holocaust.* Doubleday & Co., Inc., New York; 1968.

Lasswell, Harold D., and Lerner, Daniel, eds. *World Revolutionary Elites: Studies in Coercive Ideological Movements.* The MIT Press, Cambridge, Mass.; 1965.

Leeuw, Hendrik de. *Sinful Cities of the Western World.* Citadel Press, New York; 1945.

Levi, Primo. *Survival in Auschwitz: The Nazi Assault on Humanity.* Collier Books, New York; 1973.

Lewental, Salmen, et al. *Amidst a Nightmare of Crime: Manuscripts of Members of Sonderkommando.* State Museum at Oświecim, Oświecim (Auschwitz), Poland; 1973.

Long, Wellington. *The New Nazis of Germany.* Chilton Book Co., Philadelphia; 1968.

Lorant, Stefan. *I Was Hitler's Prisoner: A Diary.* G. P. Putnam's Sons, New York; 1935.

Manvell, Roger, and Fraenkel, Heinrich. *The Canaris Conspiracy: The Secret Resistance to Hitler in the German Army.* David McKay Co., New York; 1969.

McRandle, James H. *The Track of the Wolf.* Northwestern University Press, Evanston, Ill.; 1965.

Meinecke, Friedrich. *The German Catastrophe: Reflections and Recollections.* Beacon Press, Boston; 1968.

Neumann, Franz. *Behemoth: The Structure and Practice of National Socialism 1933-1944.* Octagon Books, New York; 1972.

Noakes, Jeremy, and Pridham, Geoffrey, eds. *Documents on Nazism 1919-1945.* Jonathan Cape Ltd., London; 1974.

Poliakov, Léon. *Harvest of Hate: The Nazi Program for the Destruction of the Jews of Europe.* Greenwood Press, Westport, Conn.; 1971.

Pollock, James K., and Heneman, Harlow J., eds. *The Hitler Decrees.* George Wahr, Ann Arbor, Mich.; 1934.

Pres, Terrence Des. *The Survivor: An Anatomy of Life in the Death Camps.* Oxford University Press, New York; 1976.

Rauschning, Hermann. *The Voice of Destruction.* G. P. Putnam's Sons, New York; 1940.

Reitlinger, Gerald. *The Final Solution: The Attempt to Exterminate the Jews of Europe 1939-1945.* A. S. Barnes & Co., Inc., New York; 1961.

Ryder, A. J. *Twentieth-Century Germany: From Bismarck to Brandt.* Columbia University Press, New York; 1973.

Schulze-Wilde, Harry. *Das Schicksal der Verfemten: Die Verfolgung der Homosexuellen im Dritten Reich und Ihre Stellung in der Heutigen Gesellschaft.* Katzman Verlag, Tübingen, Germany; 1969.

Siebert, J. G. *The Re-Making of German Youth.* I. N. G. Publications Ltd., London; 1945.

Snyder, Louis L. *Encyclopedia of the Third Reich.* McGraw-Hill Book Co., New York; 1976.

Steakley, James D. *The Homosexual Emancipation Movement in Germany.* Arno Press, New York; 1975.

Waite, Robert G. L., ed. *Hitler and Nazi Germany.* Holt, Rinehart and Winston, New York; 1969.

———. *The Psychopathic God: Adolf Hitler.* Basic Books, Inc., New York; 1977.

Wheeler-Bennett, John W. *The Nemesis of Power: The German Army in Politics 1918-1945.* Macmillan & Co., New York; 1964.

World Committee for the Victims of Fascism. *Brown Book of the Hitler Terror.* Alfred A. Knopf, New York; 1933.

Index

Abshagen, Karl, 61
Abwehr, 59, 61, 62, 72
Adonis-Diele, 22
Allen, William Sheridan, 49
Amidst a Nightmare of Crime, 147
Anatomy of the SS State, 74
Anschluss, 121
Anti-Semitism, 15-16, 24, 25, 37, 39-40, 41, 42, 105, 121, 128
Armed Forces, German, 36, 91-95, 133
Artz, Frederick B., 20
Atrocity, 146
Auschwitz, 114, 129, 143, 145-51
Authoritarianism, 50

Bad Wiessee, 89, 98
Barbu, Zevedei, 29
Beer Hall Putsch, 82
Behemoth, 120
Bent, 127-28
Berger, Gottlob, 124-25
Berlin University, 122
Birds of Passage, *See Wandervögel*
Bisexuality, 22, 23, 31, 56, 62, 63, 94
Black Guard, *See* SS
Black Order, *See* SS
Black Triangle, 131
Bleuel, Hans Peter, 29, 41, 85, 96, 125
Blomberg, Werner von, 60, 91-92, 98
Blood Purge, 24-25, 54-55, 63-64, 70, 79, 81, 86, 90, 91-100, 107-8, 119, 122, 124, 134, 154, 161
Blood Purge speech, 107-8, 112
Blue Triangle, 131
Blüher, Hans, 39, 41, 118
Blutkitt, 131
Book burning, 25, 103-5
Bormann, Martin, 87-88, 138
Bramsted, Ernest K., 129
Brand, Adolf, 105

Brauchitsch, Walther von, 95
Brotherhood of the trenches, 68
Brown Book of the Hitler Terror, 104
Brownhouse, 98, 134
Brown Triangle, 131
Brückner, Wilhelm, 56, 158
Brüning, Heinrich, 77
Buchenwald, 129, 141

Canaris, Wilhelm, 59, 61, 62, 72
Cannibalism, 149
Charakter Konstellation, 81
Circumcision, 31, 132-33
Civil police, 124, 125, 133
Clemenceau, Georges, 14
Columbia House, 134
Communist Party, 72, 105
Concentration camps,
  civilian inmates, 131
  first established, 129
  Levels I, II, III, 123-24
Cramm, Gottfried, 63
Crystal Night, 58-59, 129

Dachau, 114, 125, 129, 133-34, 138
Dadaism, 15, 31
Das Schwarze Korps, 64, 106, 115
Davidson, Michael, 19-22, 25-26
Death's Head units, 48
Defense Echelon, *See* SS
Denazification, 95
Der Fuehrer, 98
Destruction of the European Jews, The, 139
Diels, Rudolf, 91, 118
Die Männer Mit dem Rosa Winkel, 163
Dietrich, Sepp, 95
Dirlewanger, Oskar, 142
Doll boy, 144

Eckart, Dietrich, 80
Eckhardt, Karl August, 122
Economic crisis, 22, 29-30, 45-46, 49
Eichmann, Adolf, 114
Elite Guard, *See* SS
Enabling Act, 35-36
Encyclopedia of the Third Reich, 123
Ernst, Karl, 94, 97
Evangelical Church of the Augsburg Confession, 113

Feder, Gottfried, 20, 24
Feinermann, Emmanuel, 58
Ferdl, Weiss, 32
Fest, Joachim C., 91
Final Solution of the Jewish Question, 112-13
Fischer, Karl, 36
Fitzgibbon, Constantine, 95
Frank, Hans, 56, 130
Frederick the Great, 26, 63
Free Corps, 31, 69
Freikorps, See Free Corps
French Vichy government, 58
Frick, Wilhelm, 121
Fritsch, Werner von, 59-60, 62, 63
Fühlsbüttel, 129
Führerprinzip, 40
Funk, Walther, 56, 63

Gay Activists Alliance, 141
Gay Community News, 141
Gay genocide, beginning of, 25
Gay Liberation movement, origin, 13
Gay Liberator, 113
Gay movement, ceases to exist, 42-43
Gay-verity image, 39
Geheime Staats Polizei, See Gestapo
Gemeinschaft, 46, 47
German Catastrophe, The, 16

German Wandervögel Movement as an Erotic Phenomenon, The, 39
Germany, 129
German Youth and the Nazi Dream of Victory, 46
Germany's National Vice, 57
Gestapo, 17, 59, 61, 91, 99, 118, 126, 133, 147
Glasser, Ira, 111
Goebbels, Joseph, 24, 58, 93, 99-100, 125, 160
Goldstein, Richard, 139, 141
Goldston, Robert, 53
Göring, Hermann, 24, 56, 61 *n,* 62, 63, 82, 97, 100, 112, 134, 160
Great Taboo, The, 108
Green Triangle, 131
Grossrosen, 129, 141
Grosz, George, 13, 21
Group sex, 13
Gruhn, Erna, 60
Grunberger, Richard, 16, 48, 67, 93, 100
Grynszpan, Herschel, 57-59
Gypsies, 131

Hanfstaengl, Ernst, 17
Hanser, Richard, 18
Hanslbauer Hotel, 89, 90
Harthauser, Wolfgang, 108
Hartshorne, E. Y., 46
Harvest of Hate, 135
Headquarters Guard, *See Stabswache*
Hecht, Ben, 21
Heger, Heinz, 163
Heiden, Konrad, 33, 69, 80, 81, 98, 100
Heimsoth, Karl-Guenther, 81, 85
Heines, Edmund, 68-69, 89-90, 94, 97, 98
Hess, Rudolf, 33, 56, 87-88, 98
Heydrich, Reinhard, 59, 61-62, 63, 112
Hilberg, Raul, 139, 140
Himmler, Hans, 125
Himmler, Heinrich, 47-48, 61, 63, 64, 66, 85-86, 97, 112, 114, 115, 117, 118, 121-26, 158
Hindenburg, Paul von, 53, 77, 91, 92, 93
Hirschfeld, Magnus, 25, 103-5, 154, 161
Hirschfeld Institute, *See* Institute of Sexual Science
History of the German Resistance, The, 63
Hitler, 91
Hitler, Adolf,
- an actor, 32-33
- becomes Chancellor, 53
- Blood Purge speech, 95, 97
- condemns sexual permissiveness, 14-18
- homophobia, 23-24, 26, 27, 33-34, 68, 85, 95-98, 107-8, 118-19
- homosexuality, 17, 23, 26, 55, 56-57, 118-19
- homosexuals attracted to, 23, 30, 33, 39-40
- July Plot, 59
- Oath, 35, 93
- sexuality, 16, 17, 23
- steatopygia, 26

Hitler and Nazi Germany, 30, 32
Hitler *Jugend, See* Hitler Youth
Hitler Oath, 35, 93
Hitler Youth, 26, 36, 38, 51, 56, 94, 99
Hitler Youth, The, 36
Hoffmann, Heinrich, 32
Hoffmann, Herman, 36
Hoffmann, Peter, 63
Homoerotic brotherhood of the

trenches, 47
Homophobia, 25, 34, 40, 95, 105, 107-10, 112-13, 115-17, 119, 121, 128
See also Hitler, Adolf, homophobia
Homosexual,
anti-Nazis, 42-43
artists and entertainers, 100
bars, 13, 14-15, 20-21, 69, 88, 99, 154, 160-161
brothels, 18
castration, 66
crossdress dances, 21
déclassés, 30, 34
in Denmark, 111
in drama and literature, 66-68
emigration and immigration,, 110, 132-33
extermination, 112, 113, 114-17, 119-20
gay movement, 13, 42-43
See also Hirschfeld, Magnus
government, 70
organizations, 20, 25, 141
pedophilia, 18-19, 21
persecution, beginning of, 25
as a political party, 13, 55
publications, 13, 16, 20, 66, 113, 135, 141, 161
relation to Fascism, 34
reorientation experiment by Himmler, 125-126
Homosexual Emancipation Movement in Germany, The, 40, 111, 113
Höss, Rudolf, 114, 126, 129, 136-39, 148, 149
Humanitas, 135

Igra, Samuel, 57
Immigration and Naturalization Service, U.S., 110
Institute of Sexual Science, 25, 103-5
See also Hirschfeld, Magnus
Irving, David, 97
Is Tomorrow Hitler's?, 32

Jansen, Wilhelm, 40
Jarman, T. L., 14, 72, 76
Jehovah's Witnesses, 131
Judeodemocracy, 16
Jugendkultur, 37
Jung, Carl G., 31
Jungwandervögel, 40, 41

Kahr, Gustav Ritter von, 82
Kaltenbrunner, Ernst, 62
Kantdiele, 21
Kapp Putsch, 45
Ka-Tzetnik, 146, 177 *n.* 12
Kersten, Felix, 117, 121-23
King Christian X, 111
Kinsey, Alfred C., 31, 42
Kleist-Kasino, 88
Klotz, Helmut, 86
Knickerbocker, H. R., 26, 32, 33, 70, 96
Koch, H. W., 36, 38, 39
Kogon, Eugen, 141
Krebs, Albert, 23, 47, 49, 70-71, 73
Kristallnacht, See Crystal Night
Kroll Opera House, 65
Kubizek, August, 17

Lasswell, Harold D., 94
League of Human Rights, 66
Leeuw, Hendrik de, 35
Lenk, Gustav Adolf, 38
Lerner, Daniel, 94
Lesbians, 20-21, 115
Levi, Primo, 142, 143, 150

Lewental, Salmen, 147-48, 151-52
Lichtenburg, 129
Life and Death of Nazi Germany, The, 53
Lippert, Michael, 95
Long, Wellington, 113
Lorant, Stefan, 106
Lubbe, Marinus Van der, 65
Lutze, Viktor, 78, 99

McRandle, James H., 37, 118
Mann, Klaus, 18
Mauthausen, 129
Medical experimentation, 114, 118, 130-31
Mehring, Walther, 31
Meinecke, Friedrich, 16, 47
Mein Kampf, 80
Mengele, Josef, 131
Mikado, 20
Moslemization, 149
Moustache Café, 21
Mussolini, Benito, 14, 57
Mussulmen, 149

Natzweiler, 129, 141
Nazi Movement,
  composition, 29-31, 33, 47-49, 107
  extent of homosexuality, 31, 56-57, 62, 87, 88-89
  idealism, 73
  largest party, 47
  as a youth movement, 30-31, 47, 48
Nazi Party Program, 20, 24
Nazi Women's Auxiliary, 72
Nemesis of Power, The, 91
Neudegg, L. D. Claassen von, 135
Neuengamme, 129
Neumann, Franz, 120
Neusustrum, 129
Neuwied, 129
New York Civil Liberties Union, 111
New York Times, The, 79, 110, 111
Niederland, Williams G., 109
Night of the Long Knives, *See* Blood Purge
1917 and 1941, 20
Nordhausen, 141
Nuremberger Diele, 21
Nuremberg Laws, 130
Nuremberg rally, 1934, 33

Pact of the *Deutschland*, 92-93
Papen, Franz von, 77, 78
Paragraph *1*, Reich Amendment Law, 125
Paragraph *175*, 66, 69, 99, 105, 109, 111-12, 119, 130
Paragraph *175A*, 109, 119, 120, 125, 130
Pedophilia, 18-19, 21
People's Army, 65, 93
Piepel, 144
Pink Triangle, 108, 127
Poliakov, Léon, 135, 143, 146-47, 149-50
Pres, Terrence Des, 148-49
President's Commission on the Holocaust, 139
Pringle, Henry F., 73
Project Pink, 135
Prostitutes, 16, 18-19, 20, 21, 22, 46, 137, 138
Protective custody, 121
Psychopathic God, The, 17, 26
Public Health Service, U.S., 110
Püppel, 144
Puppenjungen, 144
Purple Triangle, 131

Quakernack, Walter, 147

Race and Reich, 115
Rath, Ernst vom, 57-59
Rauschning, Hermann, 57, 74, 75
Ravensbrück, 126
Red Triangle, 131
Reichstag fire, 65
Re-Making of German Youth, The, 42
Reparation for homosexuals, 109
Rise and Fall of Nazi Germany, The, 72
Röhm, Ernst, 23, 24, 26, 50-51, 55, 63-65, 69-70, 72, 76-101, 105-7, 122, 154
Röhm Purge, *See* Blood Purge
Röhm Putsch, *See* Blood Purge
Röhm's Avengers, 107
Rossbach, Gerhard, 69, 83
Ryder, A. J., 47

SA (Storm Troops), 23, 26, 31, 36, 38, 42-43, 48, 50-51, 53-55, 63-64, 68-74, 76-79, 81, 82-101, 107, 133-34
Sachsenhausen, 63, 129, 135, 136, 138, 168-69
Sakrausky, Oskar, 113
Salomon, Franz Pfeffer von, 83-84
Schacht, Hjalmar, 56
Schill Youth, 69
Schirach, Baldur von, 56
Schleicher, Kurt von, 64, 65, 66, 68, 77, 87
Schmidt, Otto, 62-63
Schnurbart Diele, 21
Schutzstaffel, See SS
Schwarz, Heinrich, 147
Scientific Humanitarian Committee, 25, 154
See also Hirschfeld, Magnus
SD (Security Service), 59, 61-62, 99, 133
Second Revolution, 76, 77, 81, 91
Secret State Police, *See* Gestapo
Section II-S, 62
Security Service, *See* SD
Seminar: Gesellschaft und Homosexualität, 113
Sex and Society in Nazi Germany, 29, 41, 96
Sexual permissiveness, 14-19
Sexual revolution, 13-15, 16
Shambles, 147
Sicherheitsdienst, See SD
Siebert, J. G., 42
Silhouette, 88, 154
Simon Wiesenthal Center for Holocaust Studies, 108
Sinful Cities of the Western World, 35
Snyder, Louis L., 57, 123
Social Democratic Party, 48
"Song of the SA Man," 71
Sonnenburg, 129
Speer, Albert, 99
SS (Elite Guard), 36, 47-48, 64, 84-88, 94, 96, 99, 107, 115, 122, 124-25, 130-31, 133-34, 140, 142-44, 147, 151-52, 156-57, 160
Stabswache, 86 *n*
See also SS
Stadelheim Prison, 95
Star of David, 131
Steakley, James D., 40, 41, 105, 111, 113, 118
Storm Troops, *See* SA
Stuck, Franz von, 17
Sturmabteilung, See SA
Survival in Auschwitz, 142
Survivor, The, 148

Survivor syndrome, 109

Tenenbaum, Joseph, 115
Thalmann, Rita, 58
Theory and Practice of Hell, The, 141
Theresienstadt, 124, 143
Tiene, Ludwig, 143
Track of the Wolf, The, 37, 118
Transvestites, 18, 20, 21, 25, 56, 157
Turkish baths, 88
Twelve Points, 99
12-Year Reich, The, 16, 67

U.S. Holocaust Memorial Council, 139, 141
University of Berlin, 103

Vergnügungswut, 15
Village Voice, The, 139, 141
Voice of Destruction, The, 74
Völkischer Beobachter, 69, 83
Volksgemeinschaft, 31, 37, 50

Waffen-SS, 142
Waite, Robert G. L., 17, 26, 30, 32, 33, 37, 47, 117, 118, 119
Wandering Birds, *See Wandervögel*
Wandervögel, 36-42
Wannsee Conference, 112-13, 130
Wehrmacht, 60
Weimar Republic, 14-16, 26, 29-30, 37, 46, 48, 71, 86, 113
Wheeler-Bennett, John W., 91, 94
Wholesome popular sentiment, 41, 66, 106, 119
"Why," 73
Wiessee, *See* Bad Wiessee
Wife-swapping, 13
Women's Liberation movement, origin, 13
World, the Flesh and Myself, The, 19
World League for Sexual Reform, 104
World Revolutionary Elites, 94
World War I, aftermath, 45-47

Young Hitler, 17
Youth League of the National Socialist Workers Party, 38
Youth movement, 22, 46-47
See also Hitler Youth; *Wandervögel*